Praise for
The Bride(zilla) of Christ

"I love the w and voices play off each other а ιok. They provide honesty, hui ness, humility, and clarity. As someone who has been hurt by churches and who has doled out more hurt than I probably realize, I found *Bride(zilla)* uncomfortable but incredibly helpful therapy for my soul. Church leaders need this book. Those who have been hurt by churches need it too. I can't recommend it highly enough."

—BARNABAS PIPER, author and podcast co-host
of *The Happy Rant* with Ted and Ronnie

"This book was simultaneously all that I hoped and not at all what I expected. Without throwing the church under the bus or minimizing the hurt that can be caused in her midst, Kluck and Martin share their hearts, their scars, and great insights for believers who may be tempted to write off the church for good."

—ZACHARY BARTELS, author of *The Last Con* and *Playing Saint*; pastor of Judson Baptist Church, Lansing, MI

"Rather than lamenting for a return to the early church through misplaced nostalgia, or recommending magic bullet solutions for the pain in the church, *The Bride(zilla) of Christ* offers insights into the true wounds of consumerism, individualism, and materialism with healing balm of a gracious gospel, community church, and winsome worldview. Ronnie Martin and Ted Kluck bring weighty m to the forefront to help solve the crisis of church members wounding one another."

> —DANIEL MONTGOMERY, lead pastor of Sojourn
> Community Church, Louisville, KY; founder of
> the Sojourn Network; and author of *Faithmapping*,
> *PROOF*, and *Leadership Mosaic*

"With pastoral care and passion, Ted Kluck and Ronnie Martin walk us through the joys and sorrows of being a part of the body of Christ. Through this helpful work, they clear the fog from our eyes to see with renewed wonder that the church's one foundation is Jesus Christ her Lord."

> —MATT BOSWELL, pastor of ministries and worship,
> Providence Church, Frisco, TX; founder of
> Doxology & Theology

"Kluck and Martin have taken on a difficult task of addressing hurt within the church and have handled it with vulnerability and grace. They allow the truth of Scripture to be primary and encourage all of us to seek unity and reconciliation within the church."

> —BRAD HOUSE, executive pastor of ministries at Sojourn
> Community Church; author of *Community: Taking
> Your Small Group Off Life Support*

"Ted Kluck is one of faith literature's unsung heroes. Always authentic, always funny, and nothing short of your best friend on every page."

> —BRIAN IVIE, head of storytelling at Arbella Studios

THE BRIDE(ZILLA) OF CHRIST

WHAT TO DO WHEN GOD'S PEOPLE HURT GOD'S PEOPLE

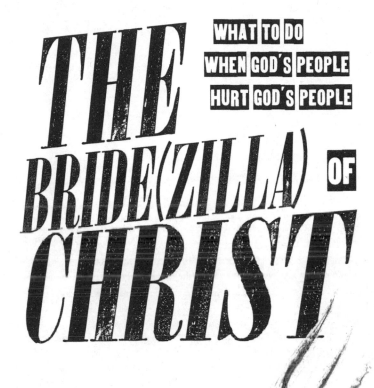

TED KLUCK & RONNIE MARTIN

MULTNOMAH

THE BRIDE(ZILLA) OF CHRIST

Trade Paperback ISBN 978-1-60142-872-1
eBook ISBN 978-1-60142-873-8

Published in the United States by Multnomah, an imprint of the Crown Publishing Group, a division of Penguin Random House LLC, New York.

MULTNOMAH® and its mountain colophon are registered trademarks of Penguin Random House LLC.

Grateful acknowledgment is made to Noah Filipiak for granting permission to reprint quotes from his research summary and his blog www.atacrossroads.net/ in chapter 5.

Library of Congress Cataloging-in-Publication Data
Names: Kluck, Ted, author.
Title: The bride(zilla) of Christ : what to do when God's people hurt God's people / Ted Kluck And Ronnie Martin.
Description: First Edition. | Colorado Springs, Colorado : Multnomah Books, 2016. | Includes bibliographical references.
Identifiers: LCCN 2016009374 (print) | LCCN 2016012689 (ebook) | ISBN 9781601428721 (pbk.) | ISBN 9781601428738 (electronic)
Subjects: LCSH: Conflict management—Religious aspects—Christianity. | Pain—Religious aspects—Christianity. | Interpersonal relations—Religious aspects—Christianity.
Classification: LCC BV4597.53.C58 K58 2016 (print) | LCC BV4597.53.C58 (ebook) | DDC 253—dc23
LC record available at http://lccn.loc.gov/2016009374

Printed in the United States of America
2016—First Edition

10 9 8 7 6 5 4 3 2 1

SPECIAL SALES
Most Multnomah books are available at special quantity discounts when purchased in bulk by corporations, organizations, and special-interest groups. Custom imprinting or excerpting can also be done to fit special needs. For information, please e-mail special marketscms@penguinrandomhouse.com or call 1-800-603-7051.

CONTENTS

PROLOGUE

I SEE A RED DOOR AND I WANT TO PAINT IT BEIGE

Ted Kluck

For most of my adult life I've been in the kinds of churches where whenever a guy is described as "really solid" or "an awesome guy"—this is sort of the ultimate churchy compliment a guy can get—he typically fits a certain personality and personal aesthetic profile. He is really quiet and earnest. By earnest I mean whenever he has an opportunity to be sarcastic or funny or even sort of baseline-observational in a potentially funny way, he never takes it. By quiet I mean he never complains. As far as personal aesthetics go, this is a beige-pants kind of guy. Beige is the least offensive and in fact least noticeable color in all of male fashion. Today's successful church man is a Beige Man.

I've never been this guy. I've never been described as "really solid," because I am, in fact, not really solid if what really solid means is quiet, earnest, and beige. I've been described as funny, sarcastic, talented, entertaining, and even "right on" in terms of this critique or that critique. Guys like me get invited to parties. Solid, beige guys get asked to serve on committees.

Where I live now, in the South, beige is a way of life. It's the color that goes most effectively with two other ways of life—the dark blue blazer and the regimental tie. These are more than just sartorial choices; they are indicators of the solidness or awesomeness of a particular kind of southern guy. They are the kinds of sartorial choices that say, "Trust me with your investment banking" or "Send your kid to my university."

I wish I could be more like this. I wish I could be Beige Man.

I say this to set the table for my own personal story of church conflict and also some heavy caveats. When my editor asked me to "open up a vein and bleed out a little" (this is really a thing that gets asked in the process of writing a book!) about my own experiences vis-à-vis church hurt, it occurred to me that I've probably been on the giving end of more hurt than I've received. What he probably expected is a story or two about some kind of explosive church conflict between me and somebody else, or some kind of longstanding offense that made it impossible for me to continue at a given church. These are the things that make for real page-turners. Neither thing happened.

Let me explain. Two churches ago, I experienced a sort of personal and spiritual ground clearing that came as a result of some long-unaddressed sin. Now, there was nothing especially remarkable about the church, inasmuch as it was your typical neo-Calvinist congregation with all the good and bad that entails: the good being a really sincere and robust love of doctrine, great teaching from the pulpit, sincere worship, and strong lay leadership. That said, we (meaning, in this case, the church in general) were kind of socioeconomically homogeneous (translation: almost everybody did well), highly educated (college-town Calvinists), and, as a result of those two, probably insufferably smug at times. Because we were a neo-Calvinist church in the early to mid-2000s, we also produced and homeschooled children as though our very lives depended on it.

Unfortunately this coincided with a period of extreme failure for me professionally and for my family in general. In this cradle of fertility, we were Infertile Couple. I felt cursed, as though God had decided to remove my DNA from the world forever because He hated me. In this bastion of professional achievement, I wasn't quite getting it done. I lost a very high-profile book deal with the most famous Evangelical on the planet in the mid-2000s. I got placed over a metaphorical barrel financially by another semifamous Evangelical. This hurt real bad and made an already cynical guy (me) almost hopelessly more cynical. Mind you, I was publishing books as though my life depended on it (it kind of did—both financially and egotistically—in a very unhealthy way), but we bought too much house and our personal finances were a monthly white-knuckle ride.

Instead of learning how to suffer in Christ and taking these problems to the cross in patient and humble dependence, I seethed. Instead of involving my godly friends in authentic prayer and sharing, I allowed bitterness to take root. I looked for validation and pleasure where I shouldn't have. I became even more sarcastic than usual. I was unspeakably jealous of good men who had more (success, children, whatever) than I did. Outwardly, I was still the fun-loving appropriate party guy. Inwardly, I was a mess.

It almost ruined my life.

But then God did a strange thing. He used the selfsame imperfect and sometimes smug church to save my life and my soul. He convicted me with Scripture and a sermon. It was men from that church who took me in, shivering, sobbing, and afraid for my soul, who answered my calls, and who heard my confessions. They graciously forgave and loved me in spite of my sins. They challenged and counseled. They were a fragrance of Christ to me in those hard months as the Holy Spirit was replacing my heart of stone with a heart of flesh.

This is why I am compelled to write to people who have been hurt by the church, making the point that the church (imperfect though she may be) is still a tremendous source of hope, growth, and comfort. It's a necessary part of the life of a believer.

My story didn't end perfectly, from an earthly perspective. Our finances didn't miraculously change overnight, as is the arc of so many badly done "Christian" films. But God provided. I don't feel amazing each day. I am still wrecked with sadness and regret when I think of my sins, but I am not guilty, because I know that Christ has paid for each one. Sin had left a crimson stain, but He washed it white as snow.

I haven't become Beige Man. I am still a guy who complains and wisecracks too much. But by His grace, God is allowing me to live and move and have my being. He is smoothing off the rough edges and using the church to do it. Today I will sit in a membership interview and tell this story to my new church, not as a means of self-flagellation, but as a means of local accountability and giving God the glory that is His. The glory that exists because He used an imperfect place, the church, to save my life.

PROLOGUE CONTINUED

UNRESOLVED TO GLORY

Ronnie Martin

B ut what happens when your story is a page-turner? When God uses it to crack the icy, hardened soil around your heart to create jagged and bleeding edges? You gasp for air, you grasp for answers, and you question your future as it unfolds in front of public cries and probing eyes. What happens when you become that person? That person you know or hear about but can't imagine going through what he's going through. Until you go through it.

It was a Friday. My wife, Melissa, and I would be heading north to perform a wedding in a few hours. After months of prayer, counsel, and very little peace of mind, an agonizing decision had been made. They say church planting is not for the faint of heart, so I suppose we decided to go ahead and ignore the rather high percentage of faintheartedness and fragility that was spilling over into everything. And maybe it was because there was a rather pronounced heartbeat to build something that God alone would have to build that provided the tiny thimble of bravery we might have had. Nothing felt very clear except that we clearly needed to move forward.

Of course, we'd have to leave the church we'd been at for years. I shared the news with the person I needed to share the news with. It should be noted that although a measure of fear was hanging over the proceedings, hope also had a seat at the table. This wouldn't be new news after all, just a decision that had been made after months of discussions, without any of the details beyond those even remotely decided or planned.

I've always been told I have a fairly good gift of discernment. Not that I always read a situation or person correctly, just that I get it right far more than I get it wrong. This situation would fall in the latter category in a way deeper than I could have possibly imagined. To say the news wasn't received well would be like saying a bear tends to get a bit agitated when you take his honey away. The anger was explosive. The accusations darted like knives. A bitterness emerged immediately. I was like a soldier who'd gone unwittingly into war with no armor on whatsoever. And then I had to go. The wedding rehearsal was in an hour.

We parted, composure attempted but barely maintained. The drive north was buried in reeling and confusion. The weekend was filled with angry texts as gossip and slander started flooding in from people who were given information we had no hand in communicating. On Sunday it was announced from the platform that we were leaving. Our insurance was canceled. The elders gave us three weeks. E-mails to friends and ministry leaders were blocked. It was an inexplicable end. Devastation reached unparalleled heights in the emotional pools of our heads and hearts. It felt the way drowning feels in a slow-motion dream.

In the nuances of these nightmares, we ached for answers. What to do, what to do? No escape, and in a matter of days, no paycheck. We became an encyclopedia of worst-case scenarios, while finding occasional minutes of comic relief in the shocking hilarity of it all.

And yet, the light of grace beamed like lasers through the almost inconsolable blackness. Somehow, peace found its way into the inner reaches. God surrounded us with a shield of people who would not let us fall. By God's grace we stand side by side with them today. And yet, even now, there is still fallout. Years later, people still talk. We're reminded that resolution is hoped for but never guaranteed this side of glory.

This book is for those with unresolved stories, like mine. For those who love the church as much as they've been on the losing end of it. It's a book for those who need to be reminded of who the head of the church will always be so they will return to Him and the people who sin against Him. In reality, all of us are those people, aren't we? We've all gone and are going through that which God is using to conform us into the image of His Son. And so we don't lose hope but rest in blessed assurance that Christ's bride will continue to be transformed into the same image from one degree of glory to another.

EXPLOSIONS IN THE SKY

A FAIRY TALE

Ted Kluck

Picture a bucolic midwestern town. A little blue collar. A little university. A little conservative, and of course by a little conservative I mean a *lot* conservative. This is an American flag T-shirt kind of town. This is a Republican think-tank kind of town. It's the kind of town where "rapid change" is measured in decades, not minutes, hours, days, or weeks.

In many ways it's the perfect kind of town. People say hello. The quaint coffee shop remains quaint because people love and support it accordingly. The town even supports a few "unconventional" types, like the skinny, long-haired middle-aged guy who runs the used-record store, because somewhere in the cosmos there's a bylaw that says all used-record store owners are skinny, long-haired middle-aged guys.

In this town there happens to reside the national headquarters of a large church denomination, which, culturally, resides someplace in between mainline and evangelical. The denomination's showpiece church resides in town and is the biggest, most impressive building in town. It's also, maybe, the town's most successful business. Like most churches birthed out of the Hybels/megachurch/'80s model, it is large, taupe, carpeted, comfortable, and well appointed, and there is also a café. This, I've found, is a staple of all churches of that era.

Into this scene steps my friend. My friend has been an independent thinker, an entrepreneur, and a musician his entire life. He's recently moved to Midwestern Town (henceforth MWT) from Los Angeles, California, where he would routinely spend two hours in traffic each evening and where change was breakneck and constant. In L.A., change was the only constant. Not so in MWT.

For a time there was a mutually satisfying honeymoon period in which the American flag–shirt population was enamored by my skinny-jeans, faux-military-jacket-wearing Los Angeles friend. He couldn't have stood out more if he was walking down Main Street each day wearing an astronaut's outfit. Each trip out for a latte he would be regarded and talked about as though he were a real living, breathing celebrity, with people's reactions ranging from "Tell us about the music industry!" to "Why on earth would you move to this town?"*

---

* My friend is, of course, my coauthor, Ronnie Martin. For a while we thought it might be interesting to write this little vignette in a thinly veiled fairy-tale style, but we realized that doing so connotes a lack of courage and even the phrase "thinly veiled" is a little obnoxious, don't you think? Anyway, it's Ronnie, but I left the rest of it the same because I think the fairy-tale thing is an interesting and fun aesthetic choice.

For a while my friend and the town reveled in their mutual discovery of each other. Antique stores were frequented. Autumns were enjoyed, and fallen leaves raked. The first winter was quaint. Photographs of the snow were taken and of course Instagrammed, and comments were made like, "How are you and your wife surviving winter?" to which my friend would guffaw good-naturedly and say something polite about how much they were enjoying it. What's weird is that they actually *did* enjoy it. A series of get-to-know-you dinners were had and enjoyed.

My friend took a job as a worship leader at the Hybels knockoff, and the moment he signed his contract he became the hippest person who had ever darkened the door of said church. While the rest of the aesthetic was all taupe and faux ficus trees, my friend's office was a minimalist's delight replete with art books, vinyl records, and a reformed book collection that made his office look like an annexed Crossway Publishing warehouse in the way that all reformed pastors' offices should look like annexed Crossway Publishing warehouses.

But the thing was my friend loved the Bible, loved the church, and loved ministry. He did his best to lead worship, teach Sunday school classes, and lead small groups. He longed to do more than pick three praise songs to play each Sunday, but for a long time did the picking and the playing of those songs, steadfastly, each Sunday.

At some point the joy of discovery waned as joys of discovery always do. This is why people don't spend forever falling in love, and if they say they do, they're lying.

My friend, being creative, entrepreneurial, and eager to minister, began longing to preach. This longing to preach was met, initially, by some opportunities, but later those opportunities began to diminish. His ideas fell on deaf ears in a town and a church where change happened at a glacial pace. Discouragement set in, but then, in time, discouragement gave way to inspiration.

Concurrently, harmony and mutual discovery gave way to acrimony and conflict. A conflict that, as all conflicts are, was distressingly living and active. The kind of conflict that loads a glance in a hallway. That loads a previously unloaded comment in a meeting. That thinks the worst of the other. The kind of conflict where the idea of grace given because of the boundless grace of Christ we've received is somehow but also understandably forgotten. This is the Enemy at work in concert with the still-live cultures of sin nature, ego, and pride that swim in our hearts—hearts that are capable of nothing good apart from Christ.

Sometimes we forget this and wield the kind of power that the world wields. People do this. It's not unusual. People hurt other people. Commitments are broken and motives are impugned. There's usually someone involved—usually a strong, charismatic leader—who has never had his motives questioned before or, at least, has never met an argument he hasn't won. He sees human interaction as competition and perhaps sees church as a territory that must be either annexed or protected, because he has been fed a steady diet of the world's constructs of power via 1980s corporate culture and his steady diet of John Wayne movies, which are both "clean" and "wholesome."

For the record, I love John Wayne, and I met and really like the John Wayne figure in this anecdote, which all serves to almost hopelessly complicate these sorts of conflicts.

He is a strong figure. John Wayneian himself in stature and stride. He was probably a college athlete of some kind. The church is "protected" and prospers. People feel safe. Coffee flows. Conflicts are somewhat gray and difficult because that's pretty much how they always are. My friend loses sleep. He knows his days are numbered. His chest pounds while he lies in bed, and the house and town, which once seemed so quaint, now fill him with questions like, "Should we have come here?" and "What are we doing here?" and "Why is this happening?" The coffee shop that once held fawning, curious admirers now holds the aroma of distrust and anxiety, which is perceived even if not actually there.

This kind of thing happens outside and inside churches

every day because we *need* Christ desperately, and we don't just need Him on that one sunny day when we're six, by the swing set, when we "ask Him into our hearts."

E-mails are sent and, as is often the case when people are in a deep state of conflict, misinterpreted. The John Wayne figure feels especially at odds with the Los Angeles figure. Meetings are held. Forgiveness is asked for and, perhaps, not given. Spiritual rhetoric is thrown around via words like *character* and *concern*. This is a time in which it's not especially advantageous to be perceived as a flaky former California rock star with one too many fast-paced ideas. Ideas are currency in some places and threats in others.

Eventually Ronnie leaves the church. He has three weeks to dismantle the minimalist office (which takes only a few minutes for obvious reasons germane to minimalism). He has three weeks to return things like staplers, three-hole punches, and antiquated Toshiba laptops. "How are we going to live without the Toshiba?" he asks bravely. This is what is called "gallows humor."

He is told he will lead worship for one more Sunday. He is trotted out in front of the congregation one last time—a congregation that is fed words like *blessing* and phrases like "wish the best to," et cetera. False smiles are affixed and held. He is told that he's not to say anything, at the front, about the fact that he's leaving to plant a church.

In these situations, mathematics often takes over. Calculations are done furiously as questions are asked like, "How long until we go broke?"

Sometimes, in these situations, people become embittered. Hearts become hard. Cynicism becomes the operative flak jacket that makes life livable. The church that was once a haven of peace and sometimes even joy becomes something to be endured.

Sometimes, in these situations, people give up and leave, forever.

Sometimes, in these situations, a man's pride and ego are broken and that man has no choice but to fling himself at the foot of the cross.

Fallout Boy: This Is What It's Come To

Scene 1:

Drug Mart in MWT (Midwestern Town) could be a setting in a Wes Anderson film about a depressing midwestern drugstore. It's that unintentionally stylized. You can buy whiskey and convalescent toilets there. Drug Mart has all the tools, under one fluorescently lit roof, for getting addicted, ruining your life, dealing with the ruin, and then getting healthy. They also have a coin-operated copy machine, which is why I'm there with former rock star and current church planter Ronnie Martin.

Welcome to the glitz and glamour of church planting. It's not all skinny jeans, Toms, cowboy shirts, planning coffees at Starbucks, and iPads. I mean, it is, of course, but you get the idea.

Copies are fifteen cents, and we need change. We're directed to the Courtesy Center, where no courtesy (or change) is actually doled out. Ron screws up the first copy. More coins are dropped in. Coin noises happen.

"Coins are vintage," he says.

"This is what it's come to," I reply.

Scene 2:

I've never been to a church plant on opening day. I enjoy the crunch of gravel under my car tires in the parking lot. I spend a few minutes walking around the church building (a loaner from another church). I smell the basement, which smells like all church basements, everywhere. I see a copy of *Why We Love the Church* (my book) sitting atop a pile of Amish romances— all of which look like they've been read way more than my book. I count four hipsters and twenty-one regular people in the fresh, new congregation.

Church planting (and, by extension, *going* to church plants) isn't only for the young and fashionable. You don't have to know the collected works of Thom Yorke.*

You can be an athlete. A salesman. A housewife or (gasp) a woman without a husband or (gasp again) *with* a job. It's true.

There's comfort in a church that's planted by a guy who's been hurt and humbled and is trying, in Christ, to deal with it the right way. And who loves the Bible and loves people.

I can relate to hurting people. I can't relate to a church planter whose sum total is some blog posts, designer jeans, and a dream. Dreams aren't enough. Dreams disappear and inspiration wanes. Christ remains and is the same yesterday, today, and tomorrow.

There is comfort in "Jesus Paid It All" and "All I Have Is Christ" sung to an acoustic guitar. There is comfort in the gospel of God's grace for sinners (of which, to quote Paul, I am the worst).

---

* Of the alternative rock band Radiohead.

2

WHAT'S MINE IS (NOT) YOURS

Ronnie Martin

Oddly enough, one of my most enduring childhood memories happens to be one of the most difficult, dreaded, and agonizing rituals of the American evangelical family: going to church on Sunday mornings. One of the reasons it may be forever etched in my mind is because it tends to read like a script out of one of Chevy Chase's National Lampoon films from the 1980s.

Sunday mornings were pure chaos in the Martin household. Whatever kind of system we had during the week for getting up and out the door seemed to totally collapse on Sunday mornings.

Inevitably, the day would start with my two siblings and me being dragged out of bed by my mom, who by her third wake-up attempt was practically foaming at the mouth. There'd be enough time left for only one of us to shower, which thankfully would be me because I was the oldest. For some reason, I wasn't very good at time management in my younger years, and I lingered in the shower a little too long, which meant two things: one, my brother and sister started pounding maniacally on the door so they could get in; and two, I used up all the hot water before my dad took his shower. The former was just annoying, while the latter was almost punishable by death.

Luckily, as an ex-navy man, Dad was able to shower, shave, and get dressed in under like, fifty-eight seconds, so he didn't need a lot of time in the morning. Not so lucky was the fact that he'd be yelling at everyone to get in the car while the rest of us were still deciding on whether we should get dressed or brush our teeth. About five minutes too late, the rest of the family would make their way into the beautiful bucket seats of our full-sized, ten-seat Ford Econoline passenger van.

Still angry about his cold twelve-second shower, Dad would speed out of the driveway, managing to miss not one, not two, but typically every traffic signal between our house and the church, which was quite a few since we lived thirty minutes away. Like clockwork, my two younger siblings would start a world war in the backseat, and the steam would start to pour out of Dad's ears like a cartoon locomotive. While I started peace negotiations with my brother and sister, Mom would launch into her own classically failed attempt to do the same with Dad.

With approximately zero minutes left before the service started, Dad would skid into the church parking lot, almost clipping the poor guy directing traffic in the orange vest. In classic Dad fashion, he would spend an additional five minutes angrily searching for "his" parking spot before finally settling for the one approximately seven miles from the church entrance. We'd pile out of the van, slam the doors behind us, and walk sulkily to our designated area of the building. Dad would be on his final rant to my mom, bemoaning the fact that "his" spot in the pew was surely going to be taken. It was.

A great start to a great morning.

All joking aside, I think my story illustrates some key truths about the state of the modern church that lead to many of the selfish breakups and breakdowns that you see littering the evangelical church ghetto.

The first truth is that in many contexts, the church has become an empire of individualism. For my dad, it was "his" parking spot, "his" pew, and all the things he felt he was entitled to as an (angrily) devoted churchgoer and giver.

There's a lot of talk these days about entitlement. Whether it's business, politics, sports, or healthcare, the pervasive thought behind all our never-to-be-humble opinions is that we are owed something. As much as everyone likes to believe this is some new, uncharted territory explored by the under-thirty set, it's not. And as we'll see in a few moments, the disease of entitlement has historically had just as much of a hold on the church as anywhere else.

We're all born believing that something is owed to us. On the contrary, gratefulness is almost presented as a code word for settling. And nobody should ever have to settle. Nobody should ever be okay with things being less than the ideal we've created in our minds. Sure, gratefulness is fine when you're feeling meditative, inspirational, or victorious, but it's certainly not a lifestyle that gets your voice heard and your requests fulfilled.

Let me get straight to the gist of this chapter: the overflow of an ungrateful heart is consumerism, and consumerism is the mind-set we find filling the pews and padded chairs of many of our churches today. We attend church to be served, not to serve. We attend church to be won over, not to worship. We attend church to complain, not to confess our sins. We simply attend, and we believe the church should attend to the space that we're paying tithes to fill. So if all we're doing is buying up space, you better believe we're going to voice our opinion over the myriad ways that "our" space should be custom fitted to "our" preferences. The problem, of course, is that consumerism in the church creates casualties. Maybe you've been one of them.

For a biblical equivalent, let's look at the Corinthian church. It was a congregation of entitlement seekers, a church suffering from an astute case of spiritual amnesia. In the throes of material success, mega-attendance, and major influence, they had forgotten they were a chosen race, a royal priesthood, a people set apart to be the visible representation of Christ in the midst of a pagan society. The Corinthians had become an entitled group of church attenders, arrogantly believing they were in sole possession of the blessings they had received. Paul gave them a timely reminder in his pastoral letter: "For who sees anything different in you? What do you have that you did not receive? If then you received it, why do you boast as if you did not receive it?" (1 Corinthians 4:7).

Entitlement creates division, lacks generosity, and was one of the major sins that pitted the Corinthians against one another. Believing they deserved something they had no part in acquiring caused them to have an ownership mind-set, and people with ownership issues typically do not share well with others.

Sadly, little has changed. The struggle that the Corinthian church had with ownership continues today. Spend a week behind the scenes on most church staffs and prepare to be bombarded with a list of offenses and complaints dropped like little bombs into offering plates and inboxes. You'll quickly come to the conclusion that churchgoers want what they want when they want it. Instead of a shared community of believers united under God's grace, church becomes an individualistic smorgasbord of boss-like demands that must be noted and fulfilled. We pay our tithe and believe that with it should come the building, preacher, worship service, café, youth program, and nursery we feel we've paid for and deserve.

It's not hard to see how this happens. I mean, hey, I have my preferences. If given the choice, I prefer one thing over another. Personally, I don't enjoy the sound of organs, so if anyone asks, I'll plead for a different instrument to be used during worship. I prefer chairs over pews, shorts over slacks, real flowers over silk ones, expositional over topical preaching . . . and the list goes on. But my individual preferences should never become the occasion for increased individualism. The church is a body of believers, a community of fellow heirs in Christ.

An individualistic mind-set tricks us into believing that church is like going to the movies alone. Theater, check. People, check. Lights down, check. Camera rolling, check. End credits, check. Shuffle out the aisle, check.

Individualism feeds our sense of ownership. It places preferences over people. It heightens selfishness over serving. It caves into our natural desire for the creation over the Creator and then makes us think we deserve it.

A sense of entitlement does not generate generosity in our hearts. It makes us forget that we are not our own and that we were bought with a price. The Bible never says it's wrong to own things. We all own things. What Jesus is concerned about is whether things own us. Whether our ownership comes at the expense of our love for both God and our neighbors. His famous interaction with the rich young ruler in Matthew 19 vividly brings this to light. After the young man gave Jesus a righteous rundown of how well he had kept the law, Jesus replied,

> "If you would be perfect, go, sell what you possess and
> give to the poor, and you will have treasure in heaven;
> and come, follow me." When the young man heard this
> he went away sorrowful, for he had great possessions.
> (verses 21–22)

This was a man in love with God's creation, but not so much with the God of creation. He was blind to the message that Jesus has for all of us, which is to find the satisfaction we long for in Christ as we follow Him and love others.

Entitlement obscures not only our vision but also our mission. It keeps us lodged in a valley of the temporal rather than the wide-open expanse of the eternal. The apostle John gave us a sobering reminder about the direction of our love:

> Do not love the world or the things in the world. If
> anyone loves the world, the love of the Father is not in
> him. For all that is in the world—the desires of the flesh
> and the desires of the eyes and pride of life—is not from
> the Father but is from the world. And the world is passing
> away along with its desires, but whoever does the will of
> God abides forever. (1 John 2:15–17)

The first step toward doing God's will is loving God's Son, and what will naturally follow from that is a self-denying, self-sacrificing love for God's people. When "my hope is built on nothing less than Jesus' blood and righteousness,"* I'm much more apt to remember that it's by God's grace alone that I'm even able to take my next breath and offer my hand to others.

The book of James gives us a frightening description about where our innate sense of deservedness comes from:

> Who is wise and understanding among you? By his
> good conduct let him show his works in the meekness
> of wisdom. But if you have bitter jealousy and selfish
> ambition in your hearts, do not boast and be false to the
> truth. This is not the wisdom that comes down from
> above, but is earthly, unspiritual, demonic. (3:13–15)

According to James, there are two kinds of wisdom at work in the hearts of men and women: One that produces good works, and one that fuels jealousy and selfish ambition. The latter is described as being demonic because of the division it creates among believers.

You mean, complaining to my small group about how much I hate the flower arrangement that the decorating committee set

---

* "My Hope Is Built on Nothing Less" hymn by Edward Mote, 1797–1874.

up in the sanctuary is actually earthly, unspiritual, and demonic? It can be if the heart behind it is one that grates against instead of being grateful for the work of a fellow servant.

The best way to guard our hearts against the white lie of entitlement is through the self-denying acts of good works toward others. By remembering that Christ laid aside His rights to become a sacrifice for us. By radically returning to obedience in Christ through a renewed belief in the gospel that tells us once and for all that Jesus paid it all.

We read in the gospel of John, "I am the vine; you are the branches. Whoever abides in me and I in him, he it is that bears much fruit, for apart from me you can do nothing" (15:5).

Wait? Did He just say I can do nothing? He did, and it's a stunning statement when you consider what Jesus is saying in regard to what we think we are entitled to versus what He actually wants us to do, which is bear fruit.

Consider your church for a moment. Does it resemble a Christian reality show, where people are pitted against one another, taking sides, and taking no prisoners in the process? Do you have passive leaders who prefer to look the other way and excuse it as harmless bickering instead of what the Bible calls it, which is sowing discord?

Now consider yourself. Will you be the first to lay down your rights, have the courage to speak up and humbly ask for forgiveness? Will you believe the gospel?

The problem with entitlement is that it robs us of the gospel, which tells us that Jesus, the only deserving person who ever lived, gave up His rights by dying for people who thought they deserved everything. The only thing we are entitled to is wrath. But God provided a way to spare us: through adoption.

Our Undeserved Adoption

Blood determines everything. It's how we receive our identity, locate our ancestry, and determine our eligibility for being part of a family.

I have friends with wealthy parents, but I'm not going to receive one dime of their family fortune because I don't share the blood they received from their parents. Conversely, they won't receive the tens of dollars I have coming from my family fortune either. The only thing that could change this reality is if each of us were legally adopted into the other's family. Only then would we be legally eligible to receive the inheritance that comes from being a natural-born child.

In the same way, none of us were born into God's family. As sinners, we were not born with the blood that gave us immediate identity and inclusive rights into the family of God. And there's no back door in either. Baptisms, communions, baby dedications, church attendance, tithing, and good deeds can't buy us acceptance or entrance into the family. It has to come through adoption, and adoption into God's family can come only through repentance and faith in Jesus Christ. It's this undeserved adoption of us by the Father that helps us love others with the same love we've been given: "By this we know love, that he laid down his life for us, and we ought to lay down our lives for the brothers" (1 John 3:16).

For the Christian, love is death. Far from the entitlement-seeking rationalism that tricks our minds and deceives our hearts into giving only what we might get in return, the love of Christ is the only kind that willingly sacrifices for its brothers and sisters. It's a love that relinquishes itself fully to those receiving it. And by the way, they're never going to deserve it, and neither are you! But undeserved love is the only kind that contains truth and purifies us as we practice it. Love under compulsion is really no love at all.

For while we were still weak, at the right time Christ died for the ungodly. For one will scarcely die for a righteous person—though perhaps for a good person one would dare even to die—but God shows his love for us in that while we were still sinners, Christ died for us. Since, therefore, we have now been justified by his blood, much more shall we be saved by him from the wrath of God. For if while we were enemies we were reconciled to God by the death of his Son, much more,

now that we are reconciled, shall we be saved by his life.
More than that, we also rejoice in God through our
Lord Jesus Christ, through whom we have now received
reconciliation. (Romans 5:6–11)

The prayer of my heart is that we would be people who live
as recipients rescued from God's wrath! As people who bask in
the glorious glow of undeserved grace in place of much-deserved
punishment! How eager would we be to seek reconciliation
with our brothers and sisters if we remembered how freely we
received it from our heavenly Father?

Our adoption in Christ helps us remember that. It reminds
us that we're on the receiving end of grace because we have
ceased to be enemies with God. Should we then be enemies
with God's people who are fellow adoptees? On the contrary.
Because we share so great a salvation, we are now free to share
everything else, because thanks be to God, it's not ours to lose
anymore.

An Unholy Place

Does any of this sound familiar to you? Does your church feel
like an unholy place? Like a Christianized version of *The Real
Housewives,* where everyone around you seems either mildly or

wildly unhappy over whether their needs are being met? How about you? Could you be described as grumpy? disgruntled? dissatisfied? unhappy? Yeah, I know, it sounds like I'm compiling a list of the Seven Dwarfs instead of describing the bride of Christ, doesn't it?

Maybe you're on the receiving end. You're the one who's been caught in the frosty chill of someone else's winter of discontent. The two questions we must ask, regardless of what side of the coin we find ourselves on, are what does God desire, and how do I obey?

The first thing God always wants is our repentance.

> The sacrifices of God are a broken spirit;
>> a broken and contrite heart, O God, you will
>>> not despise. (Psalm 51:17)

At the heart of our sin nature is the belief that we deserve what we have and that people owe us what we think we deserve. This might be how everything else works, but God has built His church to be something entirely different. The church is not a pretty place. It's actually a community of murderous, idolatrous, prideful, self-centered saints who have been washed clean by the blood of the Savior. That's a continual washing, by the way. Although we are saved only once for salvation, the blood of Christ continues to cleanse us through our sanctification, which is the process God uses to make Christ's bride (the church) more like Christ.

So sanctification happens through confession and repentance. In other words, the Holy Spirit convicts us, we confess our sin, and He cleanses us from it. Something beautiful happens as that process unfolds in our lives. We begin to feel exposed, vulnerable, humbled, and—are you ready?—grateful. God changes us into people who are continually becoming less about ourselves and more about Him. What follows is what we see from the early church in the book of Acts. A humble church that wholeheartedly shared their blessings with eagerness and joy. In short, a repentant church. Think about it. The reason we push away from others and demand our own way is not usually because we've taken the time to develop close, meaningful relationships. Most of the time it's because we keep people at arm's length, letting fear and distrust replace faith and dependence. I'm usually not very generous toward people I fear. I tend to build walls.

And this is how we get to a fear-free zone. We repent of our entitlements. We get rid of the idols that bind and blind us. We immerse ourselves in God's Word. We seek ways to serve our brothers and sisters without looking for anything in return. We seek out those we have offended or have offended us. We pray that God would infuse His gratefulness in us. We pray that God would make Himself more desirable and lovely than the things we feel we deserve. In short, we become a people who are constantly dropping their guard and pleading with God for the grace to keep it there.

3

TYPES OF HURT

Ted Kluck

I remember a time, a little over a decade ago, when it was really cool and interesting for certain types of people at a church to screen a copy of Johnny Cash's video for the song "Hurt," which was a remake of a song originally written and performed by Trent Reznor and Nine Inch Nails (who were a '90s industro-pop-punk band that probably nobody in your church would listen to under normal circumstances). Still, when the Cash version was screened it was sort of requisite to sit there with a pained, deep-looking furrow to your brow and then comment on how beautifully ironic it was for this old country music legend to sing so openly and honestly about hurting. And then, undoubtedly, somebody would say something like, "Yeah. We need more of this in the church." Nobody really knew what he meant by "this," but you knew that disagreeing wasn't really an option in this context. Does "this" mean actual pain? Does it sort of mean *acknowledging* the pain?

The one guy with tattoos and/or white-guy dreadlocks would nod enthusiastically. The majority of the audience, in khaki pants, would just sort of nod uncomfortably, cognizant of the fact that hurt existed/exists in the church but at the same time not superpumped to talk about it, and wondering why/how it came to be that the country star whom they remember as a junkie was in their church (via a wheeled-in DVD player and sad "AV Room" television) telling them how to acknowledge and deal with "hurt," by singing a song originally written by an apparent apostate (Reznor) who used to go to the best Christian college in the Midwest (Wheaton), which is where you really want your kids to go. It was all so confusing.

Of course, the Johnny Cash "Hurt" video era lasted only a couple of years. And, like all cultural trends, it really was a way for the viewer to increase his or her social currency (i.e., "I'm familiar with Johnny Cash; think of me as cool") while at the same time making people think. In the '90s (and for evangelicalism I include the first part of the 2000s in the '90s), it was important to "make people think," even though making people think often involved not actually leading them anywhere.

And so even though I'm making fun of the Cash video scenario—which really was a funny/unique part of being a part of the church in the '90s—there is a real situation in which we don't want to deal with "hurt" within the walls of our congregations. And while it seems kind of fey and '90s and not Reformed to talk about hurt, to not talk about it is to deny a very real part of life in a church. People get hurt. Church isn't Utopia. You don't love everybody all the time. People do horrible things to each other in churches, yet we are called to be a part of churches.

C. S. Lewis wrote, "It was one of the Wesleys, I think, who said that the New Testament knows nothing of solitary religion. We are forbidden to neglect the assembling of ourselves together."[1]

Even given what Lewis wrote, it's tempting to think we can replace this special, unique, God-ordained membership with the kinds of cheap associations offered by a culture of constant "togetherness." We live in a world of one-off digital "friendships," where the only requirement for membership is a "follow" or a "like." There exists a never-ending loop of online noise in our lives such that when we are actually alone we don't know what to do. And when we are actually in real, life-giving community and relationship with people, we often don't know what to do there either. The Internet and social media give us the chance to be alone in a crowded room, where the crowded room gives an illusion of community.

We need real, life-giving, body-of-Christ-type relationships now more than ever. But what do we do when it hurts?

Everything's Fine

There were a few years in the '90s when female vocal cater-wauling was a "thing" musically (think Tracy Bonham, The Cranberries, and so on). There was this song called "Mother Mother" by Tracy Bonham in which she caterwauled about how, as the subhead suggests, everything is fine in a way that suggests that actually everything isn't fine. That reminds me of the church sometimes.

The problem with writing about a topic like hurt in the church is that you can either wallow in it, cynically seeking out the negative and then picking at it like a fresh wound, or you can gloss over it and pretend it's not there. I have, historically, been an "it's not there" guy. The challenge with a book like this is to talk about it in such a way that the conflicts are faithfully archived and validated, but in such a way as to ultimately point the reader toward the restorative hope that is ours in Christ and in the gospel.

I think one of the pitfalls here is the feeling that if you've been hurt (or perhaps even done the hurting) in a church context, then you no longer belong in church. This couldn't be further from the truth, because getting hurt and also doing some hurting is part of the gig of being human. If you've been alive very long, you've hurt someone. Church-related hurts can take many forms, but I'll discuss two of the big ones.

First, sometimes we disagree and part ways over matters of *theology*. For example, we might have conflicts over what we believe about the authority of Scripture, what our thoughts are on the sacraments, or how we view mankind in light of Christ. These are core values or nonnegotiables.

But often we part ways over *personal differences* that are somehow couched as theological differences because we've elevated them and wrongly placed them in the space that should be reserved for theology.

A friend of ours tried to start a Bible study for working women in a midsized, neo-Reformed midwestern church. The church is, in most ways, really healthy and fantastic. The church's lay leadership is, across the board, mature, thoughtful, well read, and gracious. It's a great place. But oddly, our friend has been embroiled in woman-related conflict almost since the day she arrived at the church.

Keep in mind that the story I'm about to share involves lots of people, on both sides, who love the Lord and still love each other. And we, for what it's worth, still love all of them. And the story is not terribly unique—it's the kind of thing that happens at lots of churches all over the world.

"I wanted to create a Bible study opportunity for women who couldn't attend a daytime Bible study," she explains, which seems to me like a pretty great idea and something long-needed at that particular church. This leads to a discussion of some of the ironies present in the neo-Reformed movement—namely that for a movement that is supposedly so steeped in grace and so good at talking about grace, it's sometimes alarmingly deficient of said grace.

"So what happened with your Bible study?" I ask.

"Well, some people hated it because it's a 'program,' and all programs are bad," she explains. These are the same people whose three-year-olds are shrieking during the Sunday service while their parents expect them to sit there and somehow osmotically absorb the pastor's reflection on antinomianism.

I suggest that other people probably disliked it because there is the sense that women aren't supposed to be working at all. One of the interesting trickle-down effects of life in the uber-complimentarian Reformed church is the reality that if there aren't any women working outside of the home it leaves a lot of time and space that tend to get filled up with a lot of good things, but also a lot of gossip and general cattiness. "Everybody talks too much," suggests my friend's husband. And by that he doesn't specifically mean gossip. What he means is that people just interact too much. There are too many coffees. There's too much conversation and, in essence, too much community. Paul's second letter to Timothy addresses this in part, saying, "Avoid godless chatter, because those who indulge in it will become more and more ungodly" (2:16). However, that would suggest a certain worldly baseness to the chatter, whereas it's more complicated when the chatter may be about church-related things.

My friend's husband is a calm, good-natured, and good-humored engineer who loves his wife and loves his church. But he's tired of refereeing mom-on-mom battles. I don't blame him. I've been the middleman in a few of those over the years, and you come out feeling like Mills Lane trying to referee the Tyson/Holyfield ear-biting match. I suggest that, great as they are, the lay leadership of the church probably doesn't want to go anywhere near the women's ministry hornet's nest.

My friend goes on to explain, "What happened is that by suggesting a new study and a new book, some in the [incumbent and long-running] morning women's Bible study thought that I was trying to undermine their study. It just fed into the divide that's already there." The divide she's speaking of is the one between homeschooling mothers and non-homeschooling mothers. It's sad that this divide exists, but it does. We felt it when we attended there, and we reacted to it in mostly awful ways. We weren't reacting to homeschooling as an idea (in fact, we're homeschooling our own kids now, finally making us Reformed-cool) but we *were* reacting to the implication that it was somehow the *only* godly way to educate a child. The fact that this issue was being placed on the same level as the deity of Christ and the authority of Scripture seemed (and still seems) laughable to us. But there's nothing funny about the way people rip each other to pieces defending their turf. I'm reminded of 2 Timothy 2:23–24, which reads, "Don't have anything to do with foolish and stupid arguments, because you know they produce quarrels. And the Lord's servant must not be quarrelsome but must be kind to everyone, able to teach, not resentful."

"I walked into the experience thinking, 'this is gonna be awesome!'" says our friend. She walked out feeling as though she was being accused of trying to dictate the content of the morning study.

"Our wickedness is evidenced in our inability to give grace," my wife suggests. "[The apostle] Paul knew this."

"So how did you resolve it?" I ask.

"Well, tongues were wagging," she says of a phenomenon (gossip) that is incredibly prevalent in churches but is so often glossed over because it's too hard to stop or, worse, is justified as part of life in the "covenant family." But just because families gossip doesn't make it good, and while the last decade has brought (rightly) *mega* accountability for men regarding porn and lust-related struggles, people still gossip mostly unabated.

In his commentary on Proverbs, Ray Ortlund wrote, "Let's all admit it. We *love* gossip. We *love* negative information about other people. We *love* controversy. We find it delicious. It is a delicacy—to our corrupt hearts. We gulp these words down with relish. But the contagion goes down into us and makes a deep impression and leaves us even sicker than we were before.

Truly, God is not mocked." Ortlund also said, "Adultery, for example, is perceived in most Bible-believing churches as a serious sin. And it is. But I have never seen adultery send a whole church into meltdown. Gossip, by contrast, is often perceived as a little sin. But it destroys churches."[2]

"I ultimately got off the [Women's Ministry] committee," my friend continues. This isn't the answer I'm expecting. I'm expecting something hopeful about how everyone talked about it and prayed together and cried and grew closer as a result. This is, perhaps, my own naiveté talking. The hopefulness, I discover, will come a little later in the conversation. But for now I think it's a really sad thing that someone this intelligent and good natured and talented was apparently run out of leadership on a rail.

I ask my question again. "Why do people who talk about grace all the time have so much trouble *doing* it?"

Our friend's husband says, wisely, "Just because you show grace to someone doesn't mean you have to agree with them." This, he says, seems to be something that men may do a little better than our wives—the ability to compartmentalize our disagreements and still coexist and not care. He doesn't take my decision to not homeschool before as an attack on his very *personhood*. In fact, he really doesn't care, and I mean that in the best possible way. He doesn't care in the sense that he trusts that we (a) love our kids and (b) are trying our best to honor God with the way we're raising them. And he recognizes that the Bible doesn't specifically command us on whether or not we should homeschool, and therefore we are on our own in this area. Grace is given accordingly.

We reflect on the fact that one of the great tenets of New Calvinism is our unwavering commitment in the essentials and our ability to eloquently defend them. Where it gets ugly is in an unwavering commitment in the nonessentials too. "There's a certain personality type within Calvinism that feels the need to determine the absolute right option in every situation and then systematically KILL everything else," I say. Unfortunately life is chock-full of situations where there is no clear-cut, biblical, "right" option.

"So how do you worship with all this 'atmosphere' in the air every Sunday morning?" I ask. It's a question that's germane to all of us but for her was complicated by the fact that the community is so close-knit, with all the attendant baby-sitting gigs, homeschool cooperatives, and youth groups that community entails. Her answer is full of hope and gospel:

"When I'm at my best I think 'you're no better than that person, so give some grace,'" she says. "I'm reminded that I'm screwed up too, and we each have to walk this road together on our own set of crutches."

"So where does conceptual humility become actual humility?" I ask. Humility being another thing that as a church we're great at talking academically about but bad at actually doing.

"If we're truly His, He's going to sanctify us," says my wife. "This can be a comfort to the wronged person who feels like the church isn't doing enough to punish or challenge the offending party. So I need to have a right view of HIM (sovereign, compassionate, in control) but also a right view of ME (broken and undeserving). When I feel my heart inclining toward vengeance, I need to detour my mind—have scriptures around that I can meditate on and have praise music ready so that my mind doesn't go to the dark places. I need to tell myself not to think those things and to rest in the Lord's goodness."

"Ultimately," says our friend, "you have to rely on the Lord to fix it. Justice and vengeance are not mine. Their sin was paid for by Jesus, just like mine."

4

THIS WONDERFUL
WRECKAGE

Ronnie Martin

Church is messy.

I wish I didn't have to say it that way, but since most of us default into believing church shouldn't be messy and then are shocked when it is, I feel the most appropriate thing to do is call it what it is and discuss how God desires us to live out our call in it. Ironically, the Bible doesn't try to pretty up the mess that people continually make of things and that God then has to come and clean up.

God stepped foot in the first mess ever made in the garden and promised He would start executing His plan to clean it all up. God had Noah build a Titanic of a boat and delivered him, his family, and a few animals out of the watery grave He inflicted on a grossly messy world. God pulled His people, the Israelites, out of a horrendous mess of slavery by assigning a guy named Moses to start a relocation project. The list goes on and on throughout all of the Old Testament until we get to Jesus, who God sent down to straighten out the mess of man's sin once and for all. There's no instance in the Bible where there's not some measure of filth and fury, and no instance where God isn't fully engaged in it.

In some ways, the church reminds me of the reality show *American Pickers.* If you haven't seen it, the show chronicles the life of two childhood friends, Mike and Frank, who travel around the country to various junkyards trying to uncover hidden antiques and collectibles that they can take home, restore, and turn into a profit.

What's intriguing about the show is how excited Mike and Frank get about finding old, forgotten relics that most of us have no idea had any value to them whatsoever. What our eyes glaze over as some ancient artifact of unwanted trash, their eyes see as a pirate's chest of priceless treasure. Because of their vast knowledge of the secondhand market, they've acquired a vision for the worth, value, and potential these pieces will have after they've been restored to their original beauty.

God has done the same thing with the church. He lovingly collects us in our fallen state of disrepair. He's not blind. He sees how pride, anger, lust, greed, idolatry, and wickedness have wreaked havoc in our hearts and minds.

But He doesn't leave us in the forgotten trash heap of our sin and despair. He has eyes to see a vision of the restored version of ourselves, the version that Christ, the Bridegroom, died for. He also knows what He saved us from and that there are lingering effects. In Paul's letter to the Ephesians, he urges the church of Ephesus to "no longer walk as the Gentiles do, in the futility of their minds" (4:17) before going on to say, "For at one time you were darkness, but now you are light in the Lord. Walk as children of light" (5:8).

What Paul was pointing out here is that they have a new identity in Christ. The righteousness of Jesus has cut through their self-righteousness like a light saber to the dark side of their heart. The union with their old father, Adam, has been severed, and a union with the new Adam, Jesus Christ, has been soldered together in its place. "For as by the one man's disobedience the many were made sinners, so by the one man's obedience the many will be made righteous" (Romans 5:19).

Someday, this restored version will be complete and presented in radiant glory as the spotless bride of Christ. But until that time comes, we'll wake up every morning in the mess of life alongside other brothers and sisters who, just like us, are positionally saved but practically sinners. Unfortunately, all our relational unrest and un-Christlike behavior stems from the latter.

In Case You Forgot

Remember who we are: saved sinners. Let that sink in for a moment. We're saved, but we're still sinners. Yes, we have a new union with Christ that gives us a righteous standing before the perfect standards of a holy God, but we haven't yet reached the zenith of this lifelong sanctification process, which will end in glory. Listen to how Paul applied this slow-cooker process to himself in his letter to the Philippians:

> Not that I have already obtained this or am already
> perfect, but I press on to make it my own, because
> Christ Jesus has made me his own. Brothers, I do not
> consider that I have made it my own. But one thing I
> do: forgetting what lies behind and straining forward to
> what lies ahead, I press on toward the goal for the prize
> of the upward call of God in Christ Jesus. (3:12–14)

Paul was saying, "Dude, I'm not there yet!" In fact, he not only wasn't there, but he didn't have any delusions that he would be in this life, which is why he stated that he kept on keeping on, not letting the past define or delay him from being who God had divinely called him to be. Then he encouraged the church by saying, "Let those of us who are mature think this way, and if in anything you think otherwise, God will reveal that also to you. Only let us hold true to what we have attained" (verses 15–16).

Paul knew how easy it is for the church to forget what her primary calling is, so he called for maturity, this elusive attribute that most of us in the church struggle to achieve. Paul was saying, "Relax, people. God is sovereignly in control, and because of that He will reveal to you whatever you fail to grasp in the moment, so in the meantime, aim to keep Jesus as your greatest, most invaluable treasure."

In the mess of church life, where we ricochet between a various assortment of church hurts, we're failing at something far more significant than sinning against our brothers and sisters. We're forgetting the reason we're even able to call them brothers and sisters. We're forgetting that because of Jesus, we share a brotherhood with eternal continuity due to the commonality we share in Christ. Has that ever occurred to you? Sometimes it feels as if the easiest thing to do when someone has slandered or gossiped against you is to break ties and run like a screaming hyena out of the foyer and speed away. Maybe the hurt from a trusted friend cut so deep that you don't know how to move on, forgive, or trust him ever again. In the moment, these torturous thoughts and erratic emotions are hard to move past. But they're problematic for the long term because this person who sinned grievously against you is someone who has also been forgiven for past, present, and future sins. Like you.

In fact, until that moment of eternal transfer into glorious splendor comes, when we will "know fully, even as [we] have been fully known" (1 Corinthians 13:12), we've been charged with a new command by Jesus Himself. On the night before

His death, as He reclined with His disciples, Jesus gave this startling charge: "Love one another: just as I have loved you, you also are to love one another. By this all people will know that you are my disciples, if you have love for one another" (John 13:34–35).

It's interesting that Jesus used this type of love to distinguish the people who followed Him from everyone else. What was so different about this love? The difference was that it would come in the form of self-denial and self-sacrifice. It would be a love that was patient and kind, not seeking any form of retaliation or revenge. Jesus's followers would give this love to others not for what they deserved but from the mercy they themselves were given despite what they deserved.

Tim Keller wrote, "Mercy and forgiveness must be free and unmerited to the wrongdoer. If the wrongdoer has to do something to merit it, then it isn't mercy, but forgiveness *always* comes at a cost to the one granting the forgiveness."[3]

So the mark of our new union with Christ is that we love and forgive one another in the mess of life. But what's responsible for this mess? It's far too easy to yawn, say "sin," and then roll over and go back to sleep counting little sheep you've given names to like vengeance and vindication. Is there something wrong in what we expect from the body of Christ? Have we elevated people to a place where they can't make mistakes, and when they do we spin our forgiveness quota down from seventy times seven to negative seven?

The apostle Paul never denied the mess we find ourselves in. He wrote to churches that were swimming in messes the size of tidal waves. But he did call for Christian maturity, for holding true to the life we've attained in Jesus Christ, with the understanding that we're all at different places on that narrow road.

KEEP YOUR EXPECTATIONS LOW

Part of living in the mess of positional righteousness but practical sinfulness is the expectations we carry around with us. Every endeavor, however great or small, carries with it the weight of what we hope will happen. We probably bring greater expectations into our relationships than we do in any other area, and even more so with our fellow brothers and sisters in Christ. Sure, we know that categorically we're all sinners saved by grace, but we wrongly assume that other Christians have already traveled long and far down the boulevard of grace by the time we pull up alongside of them. When we experience the crushing realization that their road is paved with less grace and more gravel, the wounds and scars they inflict on the skin of our hearts are not insignificant. So expectations matter, but they need to be monitored. And our monitor needs to be the high-definition resolution of God's grace because we typically expect far more out of those who claim the name of Christ than is reasonable or righteous.

We naturally carry different expectations for unbelievers. When an unbelieving coworker gossips about us at work, a boss treats us unfairly, a neighbor is unkind, a family member is unforgiving, a roommate is rude, or a friend is dishonest, we find it incredibly hurtful but not altogether surprising. Let me qualify here: nonbelievers certainly have the ability not to gossip and to be fair, kind, forgiving, nice, and honest. But when they aren't, we understand that it's because the Holy Spirit doesn't have a sanctifying presence in their hearts, which is where we find the hollow root of all sinful behavior.

What is surprising is how shocked we are when the church mimics the world's behavior. The apostle Paul spoke to this very dilemma in the book of Romans when he said, "For I delight in the law of God, in my inner being, but I see in my members another law waging war against the law of my mind and making me captive to the law of sin that dwells in my members. Wretched man that I am! Who will deliver me from this body of death?" (7:22–24).

Our delight in God is always waging war with our desire to sin, and our sin still wins. Kind of a lot. How many times have you found yourself struggling with the same sin over and over?

Doesn't it usually come at a time when you think you've made so much progress? I can't count how many times I've gone into meetings with challenging church members, praying for an abundance of mercy and grace, only to leave the meeting having failed miserably to extend much of either. Our expectations of others' lack of perfection should be considered only after we evaluate our own.

GREAT EXPECTATIONS

A small peek into the world of A-list celebrity pastors over the past year or so reveals some sad and sudden declines into what many in the church would agree are messy and disqualifying behaviors. Men who have had an undeniably good and godly impact on the kingdom have been forced to exit their ministries due to poor leadership choices and marital infidelity. The rest of us in the evangelical community are understandably shocked, confused, and devastated, but why is that? Well, first off because the church is a family, and families are affected when a member goes astray or treats other family members poorly. Paul told the Corinthian church that "if one member suffers, all suffer together; if one member is honored, all rejoice together" (1 Corinthians 12:26).

Second, it hurts because our expectations have been shattered. We place a greater responsibility on those God has called to a higher and more visible position of church leadership. We count on them to be exemplary models of Christlike leadership, impeccable morality, and gospel-influenced motivations. Well, shouldn't we? I think we should! The book of 1 Timothy lays out the qualifications for elders, and the expectations are high! The men God has chosen to shepherd His sheep are required to fulfill these qualifications, not perfectly, but in a way that maintains a godly reputation so that the name of Christ and His bride are not damaged or stained.

So when men with very visible platforms fall from grace, we're rightfully saddened. But honestly, the majority of us carry on with our lives only marginally affected. What we're much more damaged by is the sin of the person worshiping next to us in the pews, sitting in the living rooms of our community groups, and traveling to other countries with us on short-term mission trips.

What we're not very good at is giving out the grace we've been given. We forget about the multitude of messes God has mercifully cleaned up in our lives despite the highest (read "perfect") expectations He has for us as One whom Paul describes as dwelling in "unapproachable light" (1 Timothy 6:16).

My point is, do our expectations of others exceed what we expect of ourselves? Do we place burdens on people that we could never bear to keep? If a trusted and reliable friend has ever mistreated or damaged you, are you able to look at yourself in the mirror and confidently say you've always lived up to people's expectations of you? I'm going to assume you're saying no, but if you aren't, you're reading the wrong book. (Read the book of Romans please. Immediately.)

Paul tells us in Romans (the book I just said you should be reading, if you ignored my parenthetical comment), "For by the grace given to me I say to everyone among you not to think of himself more highly than he ought to think, but to think with sober judgment, each according to the measure of faith that God has assigned" (12:3). We must manage our expectations under the banner of humility that comes only from a distinct understanding of and personal experience with the transforming power of God's grace. If we don't, we will become people who think more highly than lowly, who misjudge wrongly rather than soberly, and who always feel as if the world is conspiring against us when in reality it's just our own hearts.

DIDN'T SEE THAT ONE COMING

One of the most heartbreaking stories of backstabbing, friendship-ending betrayal in all of Scripture is that of Judas Iscariot, the disciple who led the authorities to arrest and eventually crucify Jesus. I don't know that there's ever been a time reading the account that I haven't felt a twinge of shock at how plot twisting, provocative, and contemporary it all feels. It's like watching a movie and hoping, even though you know how it ends, that just maybe something will change and the outcome will be different.

What we do know about Judas is that he was handpicked by Jesus to be one of His twelve disciples. He was chosen very specifically to be part of a close-knit community group of future church planters and church leaders who traveled full time with Jesus, received training by Him, and were even sent out in pairs on short-term mission trips to preach the gospel and heal the sick. Everything looked good from both the outside and the inside. God was establishing His kingdom by sending Jesus to Earth, and Jesus in turn sent His followers in all directions to further His kingdom agenda on the earth. They learned community, life-on-life discipleship, and missional living, all things that became a model for future church leadership, discipleship, and mission, officially launched in Matthew 28 as the Great Commission. As far as anybody could see, Judas was a fully devoted disciple of Jesus, sacrificing his life alongside the other disciples for the sake of the gospel. But it wasn't really true. He had deceived them.

On the night before Jesus's death, Judas sat down with Jesus and the other eleven disciples to celebrate the Passover feast. At some point Jesus mentioned that one of them was going to betray Him. As you can imagine, there was an immediate uproar. The disciples were shocked! So shocked that they started asking, "Is it me?" Nobody stood up, pointed at Judas, and said, "It's him, isn't it? I always knew he was a dirty, good-for-nothing, yellow-belly double-crosser." But Jesus knew. And when it was finally revealed that Judas was the culprit, the rest of them must have felt some measure of disbelief (relief, perhaps?), and confusion over what had just happened. Their expectation of Judas had been shattered. Here was the first visible crack in the band of brotherhood that had been the twelve disciples.

And that's what happens to us when we've been hurt, betrayed, and emotionally injured by a brother or sister in Christ. We feel as though there's been a break—because there has been. A relational tie has been severed. A trust has been broken. It shocks us into reality, and our immediate reaction is usually some measure of bitterness, confusion, and anger.

Maybe this describes something similar that happened to you. Maybe you became involved in a new church, or maybe it's the one you grew up in or have attended for years. Sometimes friendships are hard to find, but after a lot of prayer God provided you with a close friend. It could've been someone in your community group, in the choir, or maybe a person you served alongside in a youth, college, or outreach ministry. A bond formed and a deep friendship resulted that doing ministry side by side helped glue together. As time passed, you developed a vulnerability and transparency with this person that created a safe environment to share burdens, express fears, and hold each other accountable. You prayed together, wept together, and rejoiced with one other. Then one day your friend turned on you. It was like turning to face someone who had a knife pointing at your chest. You never saw it coming. Shock, confusion, and a million questions produce few answers and almost zero conclusions. As it was for the eleven disciples, it's impossible to be unaffected. The fact is that anytime we make friends with another human being, even a Jesus-loving, Bible-reading, ministry-serving member of Christ's body, we're still making friends with a sinner who has the potential of sinning grievously against us.

But wasn't Judas an unbeliever, you ask? Someone who had a professed faith but not a saving faith? Wasn't he really an impostor, someone who tagged along with Jesus in hopes of gaining wealth and status? Yes, but what we're trying to get to is the fact that Judas had developed deep relationships with eleven men; therefore, we shouldn't think that his betrayal and sudden death by suicide left them unaffected. Nor should we discount that it's possible that the people who betray us may not have a saving faith. If the apostles were susceptible to deception, we, too, can be deceived by those who wear sheep's clothing.

Sometimes we get a partial picture of people in our lives and it's not until something goes sour that a fuller portrait of their lives is revealed. Because church is full of messy sinners, and sin creates unpredictability, we can't prevent the possibility that somebody might betray us. Most of the time, if we're ever able to achieve clarity at all, it doesn't happen until we're on what I like to call the downside of hindsight.

DOWNSIDES

I remember it like it was yesterday. I was asked to meet with the senior and executive pastors of the church I was on staff with at the time. To say that things were not going well would be an understatement. I was at a place where it felt as if I were frantically trying to stay afloat in the deep end of the pool, paddling furiously and gasping for air.

Like anybody who has ever uprooted his or her life to pursue a new job in a new town, I knew there were risks involved for both me and my family. Nevertheless, we had come to this church in good, and not so good, faith and were presented with a picture of ministry that looked comfortably similar to the one we had left.

Unfortunately it wasn't long before the bright colors we'd been brushed with upon arrival started to fade rapidly and lose much of their initial luster. To be fair, ministry (as well as many other vocations) can be like that. You can know only so much when you pull into a new settlement and hitch your wagon to a camp full of early settlers. A church staff is not going to unload every negative thing that's ever transpired behind the double doors and under the steeple. They're going to tell you about the growth, the victories, the well-fought and hard-won battles they've engaged in while holding the torch of the gospel high. We were under no illusion that we were about to enter some Willy Wonka factory of beautiful, edible, utopian delights, but we also couldn't have known that we were about to be enveloped under a canopy of unhealthiness.

Almost minutes after landing, I started witnessing some cracks. Many were relational. This was an old church in an old town, so there was a level of suspicion, combined with a lack of straightforward, honest dialogue that allowed competitiveness and passive aggression to rule the atmosphere. An ever-increasing level of joylessness and bitterness permeated the staff, as everyone toiled away in his or her own corner of the facility without so much as a shrug about what anybody else was doing. It seemed as if every day there was an ever-increasing amount of hushed, unhappy whisperings in the hallways, and back-room meetings filled with maneuvering and manipulating. This was a church reeling from leadership neglect, elders not shepherding, and an overabundance of faceless committees making behind-the-scenes decisions that felt cold and clinical.

Less than a year in, I felt trapped in nothing less than a stifling, claustrophobic, and untenable environment. As time passed, I tried to share my concerns, but they always seemed to be interpreted as competition or unsubstantiated claims. I had good relationships with some of the elders, but most of them shrugged at me indifferently, refusing to believe there could possibly be anything wrong or dysfunctional within the staff. "He needs to get happy or get out" were the words I was famously told about another pastor who had been struggling there for many years. I knew God hadn't called me to waste away in the same predicament, growing in frustration and bitterness. But I was wavering back and forth about what I should do, even though my circumstances seemed to be making it fairly clear.

So there I was, being drilled by the executive pastor, who was leveling things at me that I had never heard anybody say to me before. It was hard to know how to answer in the moment. This was a full-court press in a game I hadn't anticipated playing that afternoon. I was hurt by some of the accusations, even though I wasn't surprised considering where they were coming from. Just to be clear, our struggles were not over disqualifying sins or morality issues but over differing philosophies of ministry, job descriptions, and lack of clarity over some problems I'd pointed out that continued unaddressed.

After realizing this would not be a moment I'd walk away from and forget anytime soon, I asked the senior pastor if he thought there was any future for me at the church. He looked at me calmly and firmly said, "No." I looked at him again, feeling the anxiety racing to my heart, and asked, "Just to be clear, given what you know about me, our conversations, and the direction we both feel God is leading me, do you see any of those things coming to fruition for me here?" I'll admit, not a lot of eloquence, but being direct was not something the church seemed to value much. He replied, "I've thought about that and prayed about it, and the answer is no."

Well, alrighty then.

You know those moments in life when it feels like everything in your heart is sinking to the lowest point of your stomach while your mind seems to be going on a tailspin in the other direction? This was one of those. I didn't know what to say other than to inform him that I would obviously have to start aggressively pursuing next steps and hope that God would make clear His direction for me and my family.

The next couple of weeks were lonely. I felt as though I had been driven out to the middle of the desert and dropped off by the side of the road a hundred miles away from the nearest town. I wrestled with anger and disappointment. My wife, Melissa, was out of state with her sisters, so I naturally felt isolated and distressed, the sharpness of the conversation continuing to jab mercilessly at me. What obscure, limited view I could conjure up for my family's future seemed blurry at best. Interestingly, my doctrinally reformed worldview of God's sovereignty over my life was being challenged. It's one thing to wax eloquently about what we believe about God but another to actually believe God when the wax is melting.

HINDSIGHTS

Fast-forward to later that year. God was leading me, my wife, and a frightfully small group of people (they weren't frightful, just the number of them was) to plant a new church in a very old town that had a lot of old churches but not many new ones. I'd love to say that the conflicts we'd experienced had all been worked out and smoothed over, but since life doesn't resemble the end of a Jane Austen novel, they hadn't. Life seemed to be moving in rapid phases. The first phase was like freshly applied paint. We went from one tried-and-true color to something new, and though we'd hoped it would dry beautifully, it instead started to fade, crack, and chip.

This next phase felt like the equivalent of emptying an oversize junk drawer onto an already messy floor. Broken pieces of just about everything seemed to be littering the landscape of our existence, and we didn't have time to pick any of them up. And that can happen when relationships go sour. Life doesn't come halting to a stop. There is no slow motion. The opposite happens and the acceleration of life forces you to leave unfixed some of the things you wish could be repaired and restored. They simply remain broken.

But here's how God started to unravel and unsnarl some of the mess and create beauty in the chaos and hurt. He brought us into other people's messes, and in the process we learned more about how great His grace had been in our mess. Melissa and I weren't given the time or opportunity to work through the damage in our own hearts, so instead, God used us to undo the damage in other people's hearts as a way to undo some of our own.

One of the things you learn quickly in the early, chaotic clutches of church planting is that you are spread thin with a capital *T*. For our new church, I was the preacher, vision caster, worship leader, pastoral caregiver, service planner, setup/teardown guy, coffee maker, and the list goes on. Because of the frantic nature of our roles and the breakneck pace we were having to maintain, Melissa and I weren't given the opportunity to react in ways that would have been most natural and comfortable to us. Make no mistake, we felt devastated, heartsick, and alone on the inside, and if we'd been given the opportunity to act on the desire of our wicked hearts, we would've crept away to the nearest corner to lick our wounds, review the causes of our bitterness, and count all the ways we'd been sinned against, in alphabetical order. Instead, God in His infinite wisdom, grace, and kindness gave us people to minister to and serve. No retreating to a cushy office for thirty hours of uninterrupted sermon prep for me! Our hands were deep in the dirty basket of other people's laundry, and through it all God was showing us a severe mercy.

As we did our best to apply the gospel to the hurts of other people, we realized God was helping us with ours. Every time we pointed others to Christ, we were being pointed in the same direction. The rallying cry was loud and direct: Don't isolate! Don't retreat! Repent! Serve others! Believe the gospel!

THE UPSIDE OF HINDSIGHT

The problem with being hurt unexpectedly by people who share your faith and values is that it has the potential to produce in you the very thing that will be the catalyst for hurting others: self-centeredness.

Being hurt shocks our systems emotionally and even physically. It causes us to be cautious to let our guard down to others in fear of further pain. On the flip side, we can become angry and erratic and lash out in ways that show a loss of self-control. All hurt causes a reaction that leads to an action that gives way to the consequence that follows. At the risk of juking you, dear reader, into believing this is all easily remedied by a few passages of Scripture, let me assure you of my understanding of a couple of things.

The wounds from a trusted churchgoer can be cruelly inflicted and deeply paralyzing emotional injuries. Before we knew Jesus, many of us came from pasts in which we had given up on trusting almost anyone. After Christ saved us and we found a church home, finding comfort and safety in the friendships of those who shared a love for Christ felt almost too good to be true. Part of our struggle may be that we perceive relationships in the church to be infallible and impossible of ever wavering or failing. We build them up to be these animated, whimsical, fairy-tale stories of undying perfection, instead of understanding that God joins people with imperfect stories together as a way to uncover His mercy and grace.

Before we let our hurt drive us from relationships in the church and maybe from Christ altogether, might we consider our brothers and sisters differently from how we did before we knew Christ? What I mean is, God calls us to imitate Christ by serving one another, loving one another, and sacrificing for one another. He asks us to not be so eager to file people under our "enemies" list but to pray for and forgive those who have treated us like their enemies. Every time we use our hurt as a reason to disconnect, isolate, disassociate, or abandon, we've not understood the forgiveness we have in Christ and how it needs to manifest itself to others. Jesus gave us a model for this when He told us to pray, "Forgive us our debts, as we also have forgiven our debtors" (Matthew 6:12).

The call of Christ is to pursue Christlikeness. To pursue the only innocent person who ever lived, while carrying the undeserved weight of our sin on the cross. This was a mess we couldn't fix. But He could. And did.

5

JESUS LOVES YOU, BUT I THINK YOU'RE A JERK

GOOD OLD-FASHIONED PERSONALITY CONFLICTS OR INNER AND OUTER RING ISSUES

Ted Kluck

Nearly a decade ago I unexpectedly received a very exclusive invitation to an inner ring that, as it turned out, many of my friends would have killed to be accepted into. We were in a random unmarked ballroom of a nondescript hotel near O'Hare Airport in Chicago. The other invitees and I had been summoned there because we were all submitting chapters in a collection published by Moody. We were all, at that time, authors or pastors or bloggers of some note in the ephemeral atmosphere known loosely as Young Reformed-dom. Some of us were a little buzzed on the idea of being invited, some were buzzed on the idea that our "thing" was finally getting recognized, and some, no doubt, were buzzed on the fact that inclusion in this very literal (we were sitting in a circle) Inner Ring might be a springboard to fame. I was, stupidly, pretty oblivious to the whole thing. Tim Challies and I made jokes about being the least-educated guys in the room at the time. I goofed on D. A.

Carson's puffy vest on a little notepad as a way to get a cheap laugh from the guy next to me, who I think now runs The Gospel Coalition. It was a surreal evening, and I didn't realize the magnitude of what I had in front of me, given the fact that I was dealing with my own pretty significant sin issues at the time.

There are hierarchies that exist all over our culture, mostly to necessary and good ends. For example, on a battlefield it's good to know who's in charge. On a coaching staff ultimately everyone defers to the head coach, and this hierarchy is good and right because if it didn't exist there would be nonstop dialogue and nothing would ever get done. Even in churches the Bible delineates roles for teachers, elders, and deacons. This is healthy.

However, within churches, and basically any other social group, there exists unwritten, informal groups of "insiders" and "outsiders." These are feelings. You know when you're on the outside of a given group, even though you can't exactly articulate why and how you got there, because there are conversations and coffees and weekend hangs happening and you're not a part of them. When you're on the inside, you feel the warmth, acceptance, and thrill that come from being on the inside of something that you perceive as special. It's intoxicating to get the exclusive e-mail invite or text from the established insider, inviting you into the inner circle.

On a macro level, for authors and pastors this happens via the coveted invitation to submit an article to a website, magazine, or journal that they frequent. Seeing your article run on The Gospel Coalition website means a sort of insider validation—you can hold your head a little higher when you walk through the civic center lobby at whatever large warm-weather city is hosting that year's TGC conference. You can slip the lanyard around your neck and wonder if anyone recognizes your name from the article you wrote and ponder if, perhaps, the literary agent you passed in the hallway might enjoy reading a couple of sample chapters of the book proposal you've been holding for just such an occasion. You can sit in the padded ballroom chair, with your plastic gift bag of free books gently resting against your ankle, and dream of an invitation to speak at a breakout session in the near future. You envision a future that includes you sipping bottled water and making insidery green room chitchat with megastars like Matt Chandler.

When none of that happens you feel disheartened and let down by the fact that there is an "inside" and it continues to churn out content and conferences—all without you, your ideas, your clever writing, and your fashionable beard. You realize that you can swing a cat in any direction and hit a guy with an MDiv and a book proposal. The odds are stacked against you. Bummer.

On inner circle issues, C. S. Lewis wrote,

The other [hierarchical system] is not printed anywhere.
Nor is it even a formally organised secret society with
rules which you would be told after you had been
admitted. You are never formally and explicitly admitted
by anyone. You discover gradually, in almost indefinable
ways, that it exists and that you are outside it, and then
later, perhaps, that you are inside it.[4]

We have felt this dynamic firsthand as a part of churches in
which homeschooling, while never the "de jure" or "from the
pulpit" only way to educate your kids, was certainly the "de
facto" inner circle. Mothers who homeschooled were privy to
play dates, co-ops, "planning coffees," and social events from
which other mothers were naturally excluded. And if you were
a woman with (gasp) a job, forget about it. You were on the
outside of the outside. You couldn't even see the inside from
where you were.

In this inner/outer circle context, there are no innocuous
conversations; questions such as "What are you reading?" or
"What are you guys doing for school for the boys?" take on a
larger meaning. What is actually being asked might be more
along the lines of "Are you theologically astute enough to be my
friend?" or "Do you really care about your child's education?

because your answer to this question will drive whether or not we can be friends." This is what's hard about the inner circle. My wife and I actually considered homeschooling only because we knew it was the conduit to having a social life at church.

This is, perhaps, the most sinister dynamic within a church. And the answer doesn't necessarily come in governance; rather, it comes in individual convictions of individual hearts. Lewis wrote that though a thing (like being on the inside of the homeschooling klatsch) may be morally neutral, the desire for that thing may be dangerous, inasmuch as it causes us to sin.

It's strange in that these are exactly the kinds of dynamics that student life organizations at Christian colleges try so hard to prevent on their campuses. They see to it (rightly) that cool kids are at the entrance to the school on move-in day to help nervous and largely uncool freshmen unload their stuff. They carefully calibrate life groups to ensure that those students with great hair, great clothes, and nice cars don't automatically flock together, because, after all, we have fraternities and sororities for that.

Lewis wrote,

> I believe that in all men's lives at certain periods, and
> in many men's lives in all periods between infancy and
> extreme old age, one of the most dominant elements is
> the desire to be inside the local Ring and the terror of
> being left outside.[5]

At my son's public middle school, admission to the inner ring simply involves having the right pair of $300 basketball shoes—this at a school that has tried so hard to govern such things that they've instituted a uniform program requiring drab khaki pants and a golf shirt (otherwise known as the official uniform of being lame). But isn't it just like the human heart to find the one thing they don't govern (shoes) and use it to make people feel horrible? If you don't believe in the doctrine of Inherited and Total Depravity, spend half a day at a middle school and you'll be a believer. Or, sadly, spend an afternoon chatting with people about their church experiences.

The essence of middle school is exclusion. There have to be outsiders; if not, where's the fun? And it is this deep fallen longing to be "in" that can make even the best kids do bad things.

This begs the question, what are the bad things? As with all sins that harden the heart, we can be blind to the bad things apart from the convicting power of the Holy Spirit. Am I desiring inclusion into some inner ring and, implicitly or explicitly, excluding others in my pursuit of it? Am I destroying or belittling others in order to increase my stock in the eyes of the inner ring I desire the most?

This begs the other question, what do I need to do to protect myself against self-delusion in this area? One could, I suppose, read Lewis's writings on the Inner Ring and say to himself or herself, "If Lewis—who is as close to a saint as we have in the canon of Christian writing—says that there is an Inner Ring that is pretty much inevitable, then far be it from me to expect my life and our church to be any different." This is, I would venture, not the reaction Lewis was looking for. He was, in fact, calling us to be different.

"We do believe in friendship, and friendship is based on common things," explains Pastor Cory Hartman. "You have this wonderful, glorious, delicious world of commonality that you share with this one other person. If you could share it with five hundred other people you would. Ultimately, we love that man for loving what we love. Lewis explains that lovers stand face to face, but men stand shoulder to shoulder." Often the act of standing shoulder to shoulder over a shared experience—going to the same college, cheering for the same team, and so on—is the impetus for a friendship.

One area where the inner/outer circle dynamic really seems to be present is with regard to singleness in the church. My family and I have been blessed to be in mostly healthy churches for the last fifteen years, but in those churches there was quite often the implicit feeling (sometimes, sadly, made explicit by people's words) that if you weren't married and hadn't produced a child (or several) by your early twenties, you were on the fast track to becoming a withered-up old spinster. My friend Noah Filipiak, pastor of Crossroads Community

Church in Lansing, Michigan, wrote about singleness, framed in the context of the homosexuality issue:

"If we are telling gay Christians to be single and celibate, we MUST uphold and value singleness and teach the theology of it, something we are currently not doing." In many churches, singleness is treated as a disease to be endured while you're stricken with it, and to be cured of as quickly as possible. In that, it is not unlike cancer. "It's not about having a great singles ministry," he writes. "It's about valuing singleness as a high calling—this is much harder, it can't be programmed."[6]

Indeed, we both grew up in a decade (the '80s) when it seemed as though Christ died on the cross only so that we could have Christian colleges so that we could meet other Christian people so that we could marry them and have Christian children and perfect Christian families.

According to Filipiak's survey, of those identifying as professing Christians, 45.83 percent of Christian singles "feel devalued, like an outcast, or in a lesser life stage at church because they are single." Filipiak's subjects spoke about their struggles related to singleness in the church. One stated, "[There is] constant lip service to the value of the single life, but lack of actual cultural follow through. Maybe one leader at the church is a single person. The rhetoric and implicit narrative of much of the pulpit messaging is pretty clear that being married is more important and valued."

Another wrote, "I think the hardest thing is sometimes just looking around and feeling like I am one of the very few singles, or times when married couples in the church don't initiate with me as a friend. Sometimes I feel like the topic of casual conversation at my community group is totally revolved around being married/spouses, and I don't have a lot to add to the conversation since that isn't my reality. It sometimes feels like married people don't know what to ask me aside from my job or if I'm in a relationship."

Filipiak wrote, "The Church is badly swinging and missing on a very large portion of Christian singles out there. The sad irony of this is the New Testament, on two very specific occasions (one by Jesus and one by Paul, two pretty good examples of singleness!), teaches singleness as a *higher calling* than marriage. Yet in the Church, we often teach the opposite."

He cited Matthew 19:12, which reads, "There are those who choose to live like eunuchs for the sake of the kingdom of heaven. The one who can accept this should accept it." He then went on to say, "[Jesus] then offers the choice of singleness as one that is *directly* associated with the cause and glory of the kingdom of heaven. Nowhere in Scripture do you find marriage talked about as being directly for the sake of the kingdom of heaven."

Jesus's words go hand-in-hand with Paul's in 1 Corinthians 7:

To the unmarried and the widows I say: It is good for
them to stay unmarried, as I do. . . . Those who marry
will face many troubles in this life, and I want to spare
you this. . . . I would like you to be free from concern.
An unmarried man is concerned about the Lord's
affairs—how he can please the Lord. But a married
man is concerned about the affairs of this world—how
he can please his wife—and his interests are divided.
An unmarried woman or virgin is concerned about the
Lord's affairs: Her aim is to be devoted to the Lord in
both body and spirit. But a married woman is concerned about the affairs of this world—how she can
please her husband. I am saying this for your own good,
not to restrict you, but that you may live in a right way
in undivided devotion to the Lord. . . . So then, he
who marries the virgin does right, but he who does
not marry her does better. (verses 8, 28, 32–35, 38)

Yet everywhere in Christian culture since the 1980s, family
has been upheld as the greatest possible good, creating a scenario in which those who lack the perfect Christmas-letter family feel very, very let down.

It seems all too frequent in our churches that disunity is
caused by real and perceived disparities in what people have. I
was thinking about this recently while reading Ephesians 4:

As a prisoner for the Lord, then, I urge you to live a life worthy of the calling you have received. Be completely humble and gentle; be patient, bearing with one another in love. Make every effort to keep the unity of the Spirit through the bond of peace. There is one body and one Spirit, just as you were called to one hope when you were called; one Lord, one faith, one baptism; one God and Father of all, who is over all and through all and in all.

But to each one of us grace has been given as Christ apportioned it. This is why it says:

"When he ascended on high,
    he took many captives
    and gave gifts to his people."

(What does "he ascended" mean except that he also descended to the lower, earthly regions? He who descended is the very one who ascended higher than all the heavens, in order to fill the whole universe.) So Christ himself gave the apostles, the prophets, the evangelists, the pastors and teachers, to equip his people for works of service, so that the body of Christ may be built up until we all reach unity in the faith and in the knowledge of the Son of God and become mature, attaining to the whole measure of the fullness of Christ. (verses 1–13)

It occurred to me that it doesn't say He gives all gifts, or all the same gifts, to all His people. This is why we need to be humble and gentle. It's easy for me to be gentle and gracious and outgoing and positive on my best days—when I feel as though I'm getting everything I want out of life. It's much harder when there are things I want that others have. And it occurred to me as well that this is where trusting in God's sovereignty really gets interesting, in that it's much harder for me to get excited about God's sovereignty when there is something He is withholding from me (for my good and for His glory). This is really what it means to believe. And I'm reminded that God—the same God who withholds things from me for my good and His glory—wants me to enjoy and delight in the life He's given me.

Walter Hooper, in his introduction to C. S. Lewis's *The Weight of Glory,* wrote, "Lewis had his share—some would say more than his share—of worries. But, having done all in his power to solve them, he left the matter to God and got on with his work and pleasures." He continued, "Lewis really wanted and *liked* the happiness which the Divine Son died to give all men."[7]

We often struggle to live our lives this way and, in fact, it seems like we live in a constant state of confusion and anxiety over what we *don't* have in a way that makes it hard (or impossible?) to enjoy real fellowship with people in our churches.

HURTS RELATED TO SOCIAL MEDIA
MISUNDERSTANDINGS

This one is tricky because it's easy to feel as if skirmishes that happen online never *really* happen, because you're rarely (if ever) face to face with the person you've eviscerated online. And as such, the hurts are never actually resolved because there is the sense that as long as I "block," "un-friend" (an interesting term with very heavy etymological connotations in this day and age), or "hide" (see previous parenthetical) someone, then the situation has been resolved. This is especially problematic for men, who seem to have a phobic relationship with the words "I'm sorry. Will you forgive me?"

I'm on a podcast with two other mildly famous evangelicals, one of whom shares a name with a legitimately famous pastor/author/theologian because he is said theologian's son. Being that we're all human, we all make mistakes and all occasionally say things on the show that are stupid or annoying. We also find it astonishing that after nearly one hundred episodes, people still listen to us.

Anyway, we said something on the show once that raised the ire of a known Internet provocateur—who also happens to be a good friend of mine. What happened next was a couple of days of good old-fashioned Twitter mudslinging. It was embarrassing and kind of dumb, yet nobody was willing to pick up the phone or even write a personal e-mail and say, "Hey look, I'm really sorry I said what I said," because to do so would have been to admit fault and show weakness, which men are usually pathologically unwilling to do. This is sad because admitting weakness is kind of the sun around which the rest of the gospel orbits. If I don't admit that I'm wrong and I need a redeemer, then Christ's death and resurrection mean very little to me. The chance to ask for and also grant forgiveness is a chance to live out our supposed "gospel centeredness" in everyday life. It's something we can all probably write a sixteen-page white paper about but have trouble actually *doing*.

The fact of the matter is that if we all (us and the provocateur) got to spend any time in a room actually *together,* we'd find that we have a ton in common theologically and culturally. We're basically the same age, and we like much of the same pop culture. We have the same Christian-media-related frustrations. We'd all be really good friends.

Jealousy- and Celebrity-Related Hurt

Like most fans of NFL football, I have gravitated toward and consumed most episodes of HBO's popular training camp documentary series, *Hard Knocks.* The program follows a different NFL team through training camp each summer, and while it has been a staple of HBO's sports programming slate, it is now viewable on the NFL Network and even the NFL Now app.

The show can be described as a series of the following shots: an immaculate practice field being prepped by a grounds crew (sprinklers in the morning), players checking into their rooms and remarking on how much they suck in relation to their palatial mansions, players sprawling in their palatial mansions, players goofing around with each other (which always involves some combination of rapping or bowling or both), players fighting, coaches cursing, guys getting released, guys driving around in their nice cars, preseason games.

Like nearly all interesting entertainment, it began as a unique look inside of something that hadn't previously been available for the general public to look at. It made the once-secretive training camp experience into televised entertainment, and made stars out of nonstars (like Rex Ryan), and made even bigger stars out of guys who were stars already (like Terrell Owens and Chad Johnson/Ochocinco). It revealed guys (or their wives) who were trying too hard to be stars but never would be, as well as guys who just have a unique, inborn level of charisma that makes them easy to watch.

In one sense, *Hard Knocks* is the best kind of reality programming in that the drama (will he make it or get cut?) and conflict (practice fights, coach arguments, and so on) are all completely real. In another sense, 2014's program (featuring the Atlanta Falcons) and even 2012's (the Miami Dolphins) evidenced, to me, a level of sad existential crisis that exists for nearly everyone in the NFL machine, including players, wives, general managers, coaches, and support staff. That crisis can be described in four words: nobody has any joy.

It's no surprise to me that the 2014 Atlanta Falcons were terrible given what was portrayed on *Hard Knocks*. Despite the presence of supposed stars on the field in Roddy White, Julio Jones, and Matt Ryan, and in the front office with general manager Thomas Dimitroff, the team struggled to a 6–10 record. The team seemed to lack clear leadership, just as the show lacked a compelling star. There was a *ton* of yelling and screaming (probably more than in any previous season of *Hard Knocks*), yet there was no one you cared even remotely about at the end of the series. Matt Ryan just seemed sort of wooden and would occasionally raise his voice and swear, in part because that's what people in his position are expected to do. Most of the coaching staff seemed completely miserable. Defensive line coach Bryan Cox, one of my favorite 1980s linebackers, was especially tragic to me, considering that his response to increasing frustrations was simply to yell more. It appeared, at times, as though he was consumed in a fire of his own rage and frustration that served him well on the field but appeared kind of impotent on screen. He seemed in danger of spontaneously combusting like a Spinal Tap drummer.

What occurred to me while viewing the Falcons on *Hard Knocks* was that I have grown tired of *Hard Knocks,* as I've grown tired of much of what goes on in pro football's entertainment periphery. It now looks garish, sad, and like a self-parody, much like this year's NFL draft. What happens on the field remains an endless source of fascination. But the mansion shots lose their luster a bit in light of the postcareer arcs of former *Hard Knocks* stars like Owens, Johnson/Ochocinco, and others who have become sad parodies of themselves. Most of the coaches and staffs of the featured teams have been fired, even in recent *Hard Knocks* seasons.

But while the show now fails, in my opinion, at being an interesting football documentary, it succeeds in showing that all that glitters is not gold. It has interesting things to say, without even intending to, about the fleeting and unsatisfying effects of fame. It shows, again without trying, that the mansions, cars, and women may soon be gone and that, chillingly, the players are completely interchangeable. The year-by-year march of the series, while at first seeking to humanize the players, actually renders them less human because it shows there's very little that's unique about any of them. They are just guys doing their jobs and trying not to get fired.

And it shows that the only truly interesting thing about the game is the game itself.

///

So what does *Hard Knocks* have to do with church? A lot, I think, in that if I were writing this book in 2008, Mark Driscoll would be the unquestioned Heavyweight Champion of young reformed-dom, with his multiple-book deals, conference-circuit invites, and sprawling franchise of hipster megachurches. We would be talking about what a talented young visionary he is, and we would be right. At the same time, if this were 2008, I might write breathlessly about Tullian Tchividjian and how he's somehow related to Billy Graham, how he took over this huge megachurch in Florida and made it relevant and gospel centered, and how he, too, is a rising star on the evangelical pastoring/writing/conferencing scene, doing so with panache, great cheekbones, a just-compelling-enough backstory, and also perfect blond surfer hair.

But since it's 2016, I have to write about the fact that shortly after Driscoll peaked, he was scandalized in various ways, including but not limited to allegations of plagiarism, allegations of buying his way onto the *New York Times* bestseller list, and also just generally being labeled a misogynistic jerk and a bully. Rachel Held Evans seemed to make it her life goal to see Driscoll publicly castigated, and largely, she was successful. He has lost not only his church but also his entire franchise of churches and is now starting from scratch in Arizona. He has endured a brand of public humiliation to which few can relate. It makes me truly sad.

Tchividjian recently stepped down from his pastorate after admitting to an extramarital affair and was similarly castigated. He wrote the following, on his Facebook page:

> My days are spent focusing on my family along with finding a job so that bills can be paid. But one of the big questions I've wrestled with is, how do I properly steward this glorious ruin? To be quite honest, I want to crawl into a hole and be anonymous for a long, long time. I don't want a stage, a platform, a microphone, a spotlight. I want to disappear. Nothing seems more appealing to me on most days than to simply vanish. But here's my struggle: I actually believe the message that I've preached with all my might (and which I need now more than ever). If I only let you see me when I'm "good" and "strong" and polished and "at the top," I undermine the very message that I claim to believe. I am tempted to hide until I am "shiny" again. But if I run away because I don't want you to see me broken and weak and sad and angry and struggling with

fear and guilt and shame, then I fail to practice what I preach—and one of the many things I've learned from this is that failing to practice what you preach is destructive.

The gospel frees me to let you see me at my worst—the me that runs away, the me that doesn't want to pray, the me who gets angry at God, the me who rationalizes, the me that knows I'm solely to blame for my sinful choice but who wants to blame others. That's my shadow side. And it's dark. I knew I was bad, but I never knew I was this bad. So, if I refuse to give you a glimpse into my walk through the valley of the shadow of death, then you'll never see the grace that meets me every day at my absolute nastiest. Grace always flows to the lowest point, and while it scares me to death because I'm a lot more image conscious than I let on, I'm going to let you see me at the bottom—because that's where Jesus is.[8]

Tchividjian's message is, of course, incredibly courageous and one of the most honest and helpful things I've seen a Christian author write in, probably, forever. It occurs to me that much of what he expresses is Davidic in its spirit—that is, I really regret what I've done, I'm seeking God's forgiveness, my life appears to be in shambles (and by all human accounts is), but God is with me in it; therefore, I'm able to live and move and have my being. And further, though I'm massively embarrassed for what I've done and feel like hiding in a cave for the rest of my life, I'm not going to shrink from what God has asked me to do.

As a moderately successful writer and a realist, I'm always tempted to rip the idea of fame. Steeped as I am in pre-'90s punk-rock sensibilities, chasing after fame seems a little gauche and I'm almost always a little put off by the people who openly do it (as is, I think, the entire point of Twitter). Yet we all do it. It's the little demon on the shoulder of nearly every Christian author and pastor I know. We *want* it, even though we can probably all articulate reasons we shouldn't.

Isaiah 2:22 reads, "Stop trusting in mere humans, who have but a breath in their nostrils. Why hold them in esteem?" The answer is somewhat simple: because we have industries set up to cater to us in such a way that we *do* hold them in esteem and continue to purchase their books, conference passes, and so on.

In general, I think chasing fame is bad for almost all people (as the as-yet-unfinished stories of Driscoll and Tchividjian illustrate), yet there are some whom God specifically calls to it. Like David. If King David was looking to have his reputation massaged or enhanced by the beginning of the New Testament, he would have been sorely disappointed. In Matthew's genealogy in chapter 1, he explained that "David was the father of Solomon, whose mother had been Uriah's wife." That could have been written differently, but it wasn't. And, in fact, Matthew's decision to start his gospel with a genealogy was a testament to how God fulfilled His promise through the weak, the sinner, and the outsider. Included are Judah, who was so depraved and such a frequenter of prostitutes that his daughter-in-law, Tamar, knew that if she dressed up as one, she could seduce him. The point is that God uses sinners to fulfill His purposes, and God used David, pre-and-post fall from grace, to do so.

If David were around today we'd be talking about his meteoric start and then writing in hushed tones about his fall from grace. But God used it to give us the greatest example of humble repentance and subsequent restoration ever recorded in Scripture. What David meant for evil—adultery with Bathsheba and then the murder of her husband—God used for good.

But still, amid all these current examples of fame going very badly for the people who have it, we still really want it. We talk about it, blog about it, and in the privacy of our own homes discuss how we deserve it more than other people. It's a dynamic that is somewhat unique to our generation because, before us, there were far fewer celebrity pastors, and the ones that existed were sort of shrouded in mystery. We knew that Billy Graham played only stadium gigs, but beyond that we didn't really know a whole lot about him because we didn't have Twitter to tell us.

In *Life Together*, Dietrich Bonhoeffer wrote,

Every human wish-dream that is injected into the
Christian community is a hindrance to genuine community and must be banished if genuine community is to
survive. He who loves his dream of a community more
than the Christian community itself becomes a destroyer
of the latter, even though his personal intentions may
be ever so honest and earnest and sacrificial. God hates
visionary dreaming; it makes the dreamer proud and
pretentious. The man who fashions a visionary ideal
of community demands that it be realized by God, by
others and by himself. He enters the community of
Christians with his demands, sets up his own law, and
judges the brethren and God himself accordingly.[9]

Christian publishing, and by extension modern-day pastoring, seems to be founded on the idea of human wish-dreams.
On some level it is human wish-dreams that make us write
book proposals and daydream about book signings and conference invitations and bigger barns. And my generation may have
invented visionary dreaming, because after all, didn't Jon Acuff
tell us to punch fear in the face and escape average while also
rescuing Mondays and reinventing our work and being awesome and all that stuff? Didn't he also tell me to close the gap
between my day job and my dream job? Now Bonhoeffer is
telling me not to? I'm confused.

This is in stark contrast to Walter Hooper's description of C. S. Lewis, in the introduction to *The Weight of Glory,* in which he wrote, "Lewis was a truly modest man. If his books came naturally into our conversation, he would talk about them with the same detachment as in discussing some stranger's works. But he had no interest as far as I could see in his literary or theological position in the world."[10]

What would we have thought of Lewis, I wonder, if he had a personal website, blog, Facebook page, and Twitter feed—all of which are marketing tools in the modern writer's self-promotional arsenal? Would we have grown tired of him or, worse, resented his success? What if Lewis had talked and Tweeted all the time about changing the industry and shaping the culture, in addition to actually just doing it?

The fact that I'm only able to very thinly veil my jealousy of Jon Acuff is living proof of what Bonhoeffer was writing about. It's human wish-dreams that ignite jealousy and dissatisfaction when the visionary down the street has more Twitter followers and gets invited to bigger conferences than I do, because I thought *I* was going to single-handedly change Christian publishing. That was *my* thing. I thought *I* was going to redeem Hollywood with my cutting-edge yet still spiritually meaty screenplays. So how come this dreck like the 2006 movie *Facing the Giants* keeps getting made? That is an example of, as Bonhoeffer wrote, me setting up my own law. I have become the arbiter of what is good and tasteful and, moreover, what God can and should want to use in the culture. Thankfully, God will not be mocked by my visionary dreaming.

I've always been attracted to visionaries because, let's face it, they're usually more interesting than regular people. It's much more fun to listen to a guy talk about a business he dreams of starting than it is to listen to a guy talk about the insurance claims he processed last week.

I once had to hang out with a guy who made his living as a megachurch consultant. He was, in a sense, the visionary to the visionaries in that it was his job to make the pastor look like a visionary worthy of following. He was like a visionary without the charisma in the sense that he could never captivate a room full of people, but he had the business acumen and long-range thinking chops to put people in the seats and money in the coffers. He had done the homework, run the feasibility studies, and conducted the market research. He would grow your church. He knew which shade of taupe focus-grouped well, and he knew which kind of flat-screen television should be in your hallway, scrolling announcements. He knew that your youth room needed a stage before your youth even knew they wanted it.

I would be remiss to paint this in an entirely negative light as God, no doubt, can use even man's flawed ambitions and greed to bring about His purposes in the world (what we meant for evil, He meant for good and, perhaps, what we didn't even *realize* we were meaning for evil, He was using for good). But warnings against fame are all over Scripture and all over culture. C. S. Lewis in *The Weight of Glory* wrote, "Since to be famous means to be better known than other people, the desire for fame appears to me as a competitive passion and therefore of hell rather than heaven."[11]

And who among us hasn't felt this sort of deep-seated dirtiness and guilt upon Googling their own name and rereading their own Amazon reviews? Carl Trueman, who is in some ways the fame conscience of the Young Reformed movement, wrote of Mark Driscoll in *First Things*:

> Mark Driscoll is one person, a uniquely talented individual. Yet he is also a function of structural problems within the new Reformed movement itself. Despite its distinct and in many ways sophisticated theology, the "young, restless, and reformed" movement has always been in some respects simply the latest manifestation of the weakest aspects of American Evangelicalism. It was, and is, a movement built on the power of a self-selected band of dynamic personalities, wonderful communicators, and talented preachers who have been marketed in a very attractive manner. Those things can all be great goods but when there is no real

accountability involved, when financial arrangements are opaque in the extreme, and when personalities start to supplant the message, serious problems are never far away.[12]

What's strange is that this "face your fears, follow your dreams, be a visionary, grow your church, become a dynamic personality" rhetoric is almost entirely at odds with what we see in Scripture, where we see a lot of God using the weak to shame the strong. One of the great paradoxes of the faith is that my greatest joys in Christ have come by way of repentance in the face of my greatest moments of personal weakness. This, I think, is what it means to have "faith like a child." My children are weak. They're insecure, they need help with their homework, and they routinely lose things. They grasp my arm tightly when we walk on crowded city streets at night. They need me. In the same way, I need my Father.

If I am pursuing the life of the visionary, then I am probably spending a lot more time creating (my product, my persona, my platform) and not enough time marveling at my Creator. But perhaps if I remove the pressure to be a visionary, I will rediscover the pleasure of the child before his Father. Perhaps I will spend less time being envious of the success of others and will look for ways in which God might use me to serve.

My sense is that the most compelling parts of the Driscoll and Tchividjian narratives haven't been written yet. In a way it was too easy for both of them the first time around, because guys who have that much success that early in their careers aren't that interesting.

6

IS IT JUST ME?

Ronnie Martin

I learned a few things growing up as the middle of five siblings in the Martin household. The first was that the fastest eaters were the ones who got the most pizza. The second was that if you wanted any hot water in the morning, you'd better be the first one in the shower. The third and arguably most important was that it was never, ever your fault.

To be fair, I don't remember my parents ever pulling me to the side to instruct me on the finer points of blame shifting. "First, do something wrong. Second, do your best to hide it from us. And third, after we find out, find a way to convince us it wasn't your fault and preferably blame it on your brother or sister." The problem is that they never had to teach me such winsome, eloquent tactics. Whenever I was caught entangled in the web of woeful disobedience, the very first thought that came beelining into my brain was who or what I could blame.

The sad truth is that the default of every human heart is to abdicate responsibility for our sin. It's not my fault, it's yours, and if it's really not, I'm going to find a clever way to turn it around pronto. At the same time, we also agonize over justice. We want to see the guilty condemned, just so long as we're not the guilty ones. We want to point fingers when we're caught, claim innocence when proven guilty, and crawl on our bellies through the Sahara in the middle of summertime before ever having to say we're sorry for anything.

Nobody wants to own it. Nobody.

One of the harsh realities of being in covenant with other believers in our church family is that sometimes covenants are broken and we feel like we've been left stranded in the middle of an ice storm wearing nothing but shorts and sandals. We're unprepared for the shock, so we react to the pain by grieving our great loss and longing for things to be reconciled and restored to what they once were.

But what happens when we're the ones breaking covenant and dashing other people's hopes, trusts, and expectations to the ground? Would it be fair to write a book on being hurt by the church without a chapter discussing what to do when we're on the other side of the equation?

What do we do when we're the ones who've mercilessly torn apart somebody's character? When we've spread lies and spoken untruths about a person that sparked a wildfire throughout the church as we sat idly by, watching his or her reputation being burned to ashes on the ground? What if we've broken the trust of someone who considered us a dear friend and close confidant?

THE BLIND MISLEADING THE BLIND

One of the symptoms that comes with our natural born aversion to owning our sin is spiritual blindness. David reminded us in Psalm 51, "Behold, I was brought forth in iniquity, and in sin did my mother conceive me" (verse 5). A sinful, hereditary veil is draped over our eyes at the moment of conception, making us oblivious to the deceptive nature of our rogue hearts, which are feeding us a steady diet of lies, including this sinister idea that nothing is ever our fault.

Reading the account of Adam and Eve after God found them in the garden with new clothes on and juice stains all over their mouths feels eerily similar to watching two elementary school kids getting busted on the playground during recess.

God called out Adam first, who said (and I paraphrase), "It wasn't me, it was *her*! That girl *You* made is the one who gave me the fruit!" Wow. "Okay, how about you, Eve?" "It wasn't me, it was the snake. *He* tricked me into doing something I didn't want to do." God didn't even ask the serpent because deceiving the human race was clearly stated in his job description and he should've actually been up for a promotion after landing this deal.

The interesting thing to take note of is this: the first sin committed by Adam and Eve after they become official card-carrying members of the International Sinners Club was blame casting. Adam blamed Eve before blaming God for giving him Eve. Eve blamed the serpent for tricking her into believing a lie. Of course, the consequences for this blatant act of physical and spiritual rebellion came in the form of relocation from the garden, lifelong toil in the soil, and the introduction of pain to the childbirth process, which resulted in two sons named Cain and Abel. Unfortunately, their children had also been infected with their newly acquired DNA, and as a result, their sin followed almost the same pattern their parents had modeled in the garden.

We're not given any insight into the upbringing of Cain and Abel other than the fact that they chose two different vocations within the farming community: "Abel was a keeper of sheep, and Cain a worker of the ground" (Genesis 4:2). As the storyline unfolds, we learn that Cain became a little perturbed when God rejected his offering of compost-quality vegetables but accepted Abel's offering of prize-winning, blue-ribbon sheep. God saw that Cain was angry and dejected, so He offered some encouragement to him and said, "Why are you angry, and why has your face fallen? If you do well, will you not be accepted?

And if you do not do well, sin is crouching at the door. Its desire is for you, but you must rule over it" (verses 6–7).

Let's take a minute here to reflect on the boundless depths of God's love and understanding that came pouring out to Cain in vibrant, radiating colors. God purposefully sought him out in his distress, acknowledged the core of his frustrations, and, even though it was Cain's own disobedience that served as the root cause of his angst, graciously instructed and warned him to beware of the potential unseen danger that was lurking ahead. Because Cain's face was fallen, he lacked the brokenness to repent of his anger and the vision to see what might befall him and his brother if he remained on the destructive path he was traveling down. God gave Cain a moment to pause and to contemplate the condition of his heart, but he rejected the Fatherly wisdom offered to him.

So later, out in the field, the unrepentant Cain murdered his brother, Abel. Again, God sought out Cain and asked him if he happened to know where Abel had been hanging out. Like father like son, Cain replied (and I paraphrase), "How should I know? Am I this dude's baby-sitter or something?" Sin had blinded him from answering truthfully to the One who knew the truth before asking it of him.

Thousands of years later, that same spiritual blindness has infected and affected the motivations and actions of every descendant of every generation that's ever been conceived since

Adam. The sin-corrupted DNA that passed tragically from Adam to his son Cain has successfully been inherited by every successive son or daughter since. That includes me and you.

We don't want to admit our wrongs. We don't want to take responsibility for our sin. We want to ignore it, transfer it to someone else, and do whatever it takes to appear justified and innocent before the watching world. We'd rather see our brother suffer unjustly than suffer through the discipline or punishment we justly deserve. The apostle John wrote a short summary of how God defines spiritual blindness when he said, "But whoever hates his brother is in the darkness and walks in the darkness, and does not know where he is going, because the darkness has blinded his eyes" (1 John 2:11).

Cain failed to confess his act of murder before God because the darkness of his sin had blinded his eyes from seeing the light of God's mercy and grace that would have led him to reconcile with his brother, Abel.

Does this sound like a chapter from your story? A time when you damaged someone in your church body but refused to own up to it? You somehow rationalized your guilt and "won" a hard-fought battle against confessing your sin, believing it was better to bury and forget than bow your head and seek forgiveness?

Maybe you did a bit of mental editing with the truth and convinced yourself it was actually the fault of the one you hurt.

After all, it's not as if he was an innocent little dove who had no hand in causing you to react the way you did, right? As you replay the scenario over and over in your head, you seem to find more and more ways to rationalize why attempting to reconcile would be the worst possible option for you. It's not as if you've never admitted you've been wrong before, but this feels like a step you absolutely cannot take. You believe the person you harmed deserved what he received, and although you wouldn't say it was the right thing to do, you can't imagine the person could have possibly expected any less. It's in these moments that we disturbingly let our action transition from godly influence and conduct to something we would probably never subscribe to otherwise. We either subtly or overtly start adhering to things like karma instead of the fruits of Christian love, repentance, and forgiveness. We adopt the behavior of our ancient grand parents because, like them, we've been exposed and we don't particularly like it.

The Shame of It All

When Adam and Eve stood before the face of their Creator to receive sentencing and punishment for their blatant rebellion, they had to face the fact that they didn't have acceptable enough clothing to be standing before a holy God. The loincloths they had hastily sewn together from fig leaves were never going to be sufficient covering. Their sin had created shame, and shame is what made them want to cover themselves and hide from a guiltless and shame-free God. Shame is what led them to cast blame on the other person when they were asked to explain why they'd eaten from the tree God had commanded them not to eat from. When God asked who had told them they were naked, He was speaking about a far deeper nakedness than whether or not they had any decent clothing to wear. The nakedness they felt that inspired them to become the world's first fashion designers was really the shame they felt for the wrongdoing they had committed.

Shame is what causes us to shrink back from admitting we've wronged a Christian brother or sister. And it's a deep, heavy, and ongoing pride that keeps us anchored to the shores of our shame.

It probably wouldn't take very long for you to think about a moment in your life when you stubbornly refused to apologize for wronging someone. Like I mentioned earlier, maybe it was an incident where you felt justified for the way you responded. You rationalized the entire scenario, using your incredible power of reasoning and deduction to convince yourself that repentance wasn't really necessary in this instance. And yet, here you are today, still thinking about it, not able to forget about it. Maybe it still causes some mental discomfort or a bit of nausea to emerge in the pit of your stomach. Without realizing it, you do your best to block it from your memory and occupy your thoughts with something more pleasant and less indicting.

Disobedience always precedes our shame, and disobedience is nothing more than a failure to keep God's law. We see it throughout the Old Testament, from husbands, wives, children, judges, kings, queens, prophets, and priests who all suffered from the sad aftermath of pride-influenced shame.

We're all too familiar with King David's murderous affair with Bathsheba, and well we should be, but one that doesn't get nearly as much play is the census that David called for the people of Israel. Joab, his chief army commander, pleaded with him not to take a count of the people, but David ignored his pressing counsel and sent him and his cohorts off to number the Israelites. God was less than amused. It wasn't that God had anything against kings knowing who composed their kingdom. It was that David's concern went beyond that. How many able-bodied fighting men Israel had was God's concern, not David's. It was an act of disobedience tied to a lack of trust in God's provision. God was so displeased with David's action that He gave him three options for punishment, and the one David chose led to God killing seventy thousand Israelites over the course of three days. Seventy thousand! That's a sold-out football stadium.

Interestingly, although the cost for David's disobedience

was incalculable, he didn't receive so much as a physical scratch. The horror of his shameful realization led him to plead before God, "Behold, I have sinned, and I have done wickedly. But these sheep, what have they done? Please let your hand be against me and against my father's house" (2 Samuel 24:17). One can only imagine the level of grief behind David's torturous, angst-filled prayer as he witnessed this sharp and sudden slaughter, which made the shame he felt before both God and the people all the more unbearable. As we saw with Adam and Eve, shame is nothing less than the exposed nakedness of our disobedience.

How about a more up-to-date illustration? Many people will remember 2015 as the year when nakedness was brought to light in the public square in the most shame-inducing way imaginable. The client list for Ashley Madison, a website for those seeking extramarital affairs, was hacked into and uploaded for all the world to see. The most shocking statistic related to Christendom estimated that somewhere in the range of four hundred to six hundred pastors would be resigning the weekend after the list was released. This would be the end of their illusory lives. Marriages would collapse, relationships would fail, and pastors would be removed from ministry. The fallout is inestimable. The only thing we can be sure of is the shame that will cloak the lives of the individuals, their spouses, their families, and their congregations.

If the fear of shame is what prevents us from repentance, a lack of repentance will be what leads us there anyway.

THE END OF IT ALL

It had been two years. Two years since I had seen or spoken to him. I had tried my best to move on. Things had ended badly, and it seemed as if the best thing for both of us was to break ties and carry on with little or no contact. We had both sinned against the other person, and both of us probably thought the other person's sin was worse. Mistakes had been made. Untruths had been spoken. There'd been gossip and slander. Varying degrees of anger, hurt, and betrayal had all been well documented. It probably goes down as the worst relational breakdown I've ever experienced.

After a couple of years, there'd been a lot of proverbial water under the bridge. The internal battle I had waged repeatedly made my insides feel like they'd been scraped and primered to death, but a fresh coat of paint had never been applied. I prayed that God would humble and reshape my heart so I could extend some godly, gospel-shaped forgiveness. I'm sure I didn't pray often enough for it, though. Frankly, I wondered why he hadn't contacted me, while at the same time acknowledging that I hadn't contacted him either. I was bothered by the nagging, scratchy irritant it had festered into, even though the minute-to-minute pain had lessened somewhat. There was a time or two when I thought about reaching out and offering an attempt at some dialogue, but I always shrank back in the end.

And then one day everything changed. It was like the light that seeps through the window blinds at dawn after a stormy and thunderous night. I was approached by a mutual friend who mentioned some of the tension he thought still existed between the two of us. It was a peculiar insight, given that it had been two years since I had seen this other person or traded words. But it was in this moment that God opened the door a tiny crack and I was extended a clear opportunity for the chance to reconcile. So I lifted the silver lid of the MacBook Air I'm currently typing on and sent off a short but inviting e-mail, not having the slightest notion of what might transpire.

Less than a week later, I found myself sitting at a sticky, sugar-coated Formica table at a doughnut shop, staring into the eyes of a former friend and forever brother in Christ, praying how I might be able to change our status back to friends. A feeling of depletion had washed over me even before we began conversing. My agenda was simply to put out one hand and wave a white flag with the other, so I explained to him how God had opened a door to repent and ask forgiveness. I hadn't dreamed up what his response might be because I wasn't sure it mattered how he responded. I just needed to do everything I could to pursue reconciliation.

The sun started to descend by the time we parted ways. There were a couple of tense, awkward moments that tried to creep in like a trail of chilly air through a half-closed door, but I let them all pass. Like any dreaded reunion, I chose my words carefully, listened intently, and spoke slowly. It wasn't quite the ending I would've chosen, but I wasn't given the choice, so I left with a handshake and a smile. This wasn't about airing further grievances or trying to claim any kind of small or insignificant victory from a battle fought years ago. This was about repenting of the only sin any of us can ever repent of: our own.

If I'm being honest (and there's no use writing a book full of lies), I walked away feeling as though the whole thing had been a fail. It was obvious from his expressions, body language, and the tone of his voice that he had not received the repentance he wanted from me. I felt as if there was only so much I could do. I wanted to own my sin, take responsibility for my actions, and repent of the sins I could truthfully repent of, but apparently this was nothing more than an unsatisfactory attempt from my friend's point of view.

GODLY GRIEF

God calls us to repentance, but it doesn't come signed with a money-back guarantee if we don't receive the reconciliation we think should be part of the package deal. The fact that we still see as many irreconcilable differences causing divisions in our churches is shame-worthy proof that reconciliation is not automatic. The question we need to ask and carefully consider is what happens when it's not? What happens when we repent and there is no celebratory moment of tear-filled reciprocation? Worse than that, what if the injured party never accepts the sincerity or validity of our apology and stomps away in resolute defiance? Or maybe she does accept your humble-hearted expression, but you find that the friendship never quite returns to former glories. Do we continue to try to restart the engine of a vehicle connected to a lifeless and uncharged battery? Or do we pack up our relational bags, move on, let bygones be bygones, and pray that God removes the bite of enduring bitterness?

First and foremost, God calls sinners to the message He sent His Son to preach: "Repent, for the kingdom of heaven is at hand" (Matthew 3:2; 4:17). The timeless call of that has not diminished even an inch from its heavy and heralded glory. Before we attempt to repent to any Christian we've reparably or irreparably wounded, the matter of first importance is whether our hearts have been lowered from the heights of our haughtiness and laid low before the throne of grace. "For godly grief produces a repentance that leads to salvation without regret, whereas worldly grief produces death" (2 Corinthians 7:10). Behind our repentance has to be a grief that's been manifested by God alone and filled into the cracked recesses of our broken hearts. It's a grief born from the suffering of Christ that only those who have experienced this godly death to sin have any hope of experiencing.

So do you have godly sorrow for your sin against the God who already laid it on His sorrowful Son on that blackest of days? Even the enviably titled man-after-God's-own-heart, King David, who saw only a foreshadowing of the suffering Savior after his adulterous affair with Bathsheba, proclaimed, "Against you, you only, have I sinned" (Psalm 51:4). We're not ignorant enough to imply that other people can't be sinned against heartily and with unquestionable harm, but our primary offense is committed against God. Understanding this sobering reality is what enables us to approach others with trembled speech, seeking repentance, forgiveness, and reconciliation. Because Jesus bore God's wrath against our unrepentant sin on a blood-soaked cross, we are filled with a great and grace-fueled compulsion to do whatever it takes to make peace with others when we sin grievously against them.

The hesitation comes from believing we might not receive reconciliation. And in these moments we find ourselves putting all our fear in the offended party rather than our faith in the sufficiency of God's gospel.

So what happens if the people we've hurt don't receive our repentance? This is the time to look back at our own sin and remember the times we have failed to offer forgiveness and how

God was patient with us, how He didn't judge us but let us slowly come into the revealing and exposing light of conviction and grace. It's important for us to have that same kind of godly patience and kindness with others. If the other person is truly a follower of Christ, it means Christ is doing a work that may include your repentance as the means for producing a heart of forgiveness. A lack of immediate reconciliation is another opportunity for us to trust God's timing in a situation that He is intricately and effectively shaping for His glory.

What if our apology is never accepted? Sometimes our sin against others is so grievous that we may never get our desired response or reconciliation from them. Maybe it was a sin so personally damaging that the only counsel this person received to get through it was to distance themselves from you forever. It's important that we understand that and own it. Maybe you spread a piece of gossip about another person that destroyed other relationships they had. Maybe it was the abandonment or neglect of a friendship that felt like a betrayal too painful to come back from. Maybe you weren't there for someone who depended on you as he was going through a painful season in his life. Sin has poisonous consequences. Once the venom of destructiveness has been released into the heart of the victim, a form of internal death can be an inevitability.

What God calls us to in these situations is remorse and repentance. If reconciliation never comes, we may forever grieve over the injuries we caused, but we can be grateful that God has forgiven us and can look forward to the day when there is no more mourning or crying.

We remember before David became king how he tried with all his might to reconcile with King Saul, who unjustly accused him of trying to steal the throne. David hadn't sinned against Saul, and yet he never stopped seeking reconciliation until the day Saul died. Sadly, he never received it. The only comfort he found was in knowing that his hands were clean and his heart was innocent in the eyes of God. Reconciliation had failed, but his heart found great favor before God.

Maybe you haven't been innocent like David was but greatly sinned against someone you've fellowshipped with for years. The best you can do is repent to God, repent to your friend, and pray for renewed love and patience, whether or not forgiveness and reconciliation is ever returned to you. The forgiveness of your Father in heaven will be your portion in these moments and a sanctifying presence for future conflicts and resolutions.

Growing up, my brother and I raced minibikes together. My dad had owned and ridden motorcycles most of his life, so he bought us some bikes and got us into riding and racing at an early age. On the weekends we weren't out racing, we'd usually practice at one of the countless riding areas around the desert towns and communities in Southern California. On one particular Saturday, we went out to the track early one morning after it had rained all night, which was a fairly rare occurrence (the rain) if you have any knowledge about this part of the country.

In many sections of the track little pools of water about one to two feet deep had formed. We powered through these with relative ease, drenching the rider behind us. But some of the pools were deceptively deep, and my brother Jason rode right into one that ended up swallowing him and his entire motorcycle! As he paddled his way back to dry land, behind him was his bike, sitting motionless and upright, the handlebars just barely poking up out of the water.

Here's the deal: his bike never ran the same after that day. My dad replaced almost the entire engine and did everything he knew to get the bike back to exceptional running condition, but the water had done too much damage. It's not that it didn't run at all, but the engine didn't perform quite like it used to. Unfortunately my dad and brother had to accept that and move on.

Broken relationships are sometimes like that. We do everything we can to reconcile, but at some point we have to move on, knowing that in good conscience we have asked forgiveness from both the Lord and from the person, trusting that God will use this event to grow us in humility and a greater awareness of the sin that brought us there.

The Glow of the Gospel

The gospel once again becomes our great teacher. Jesus, the only innocent man who ever lived, was mocked, beaten, slandered, and killed by people whose only appropriate response to Him should have been falling on their knees begging for forgiveness. The gospel shows us that we didn't earn our forgiveness, but it was forwarded to us by the only person in human history who didn't have to repent. Jesus faced unimaginable shame on the cross so that we could be set free from ours. Whenever we feel as though we can rationalize unrepentance to others, it shows we have forgotten the forgiveness given to us by the sacrifice made for us.

The gospel pries open our eyes and allows us to finally glimpse the true wretchedness of our sin in all its damning and depraved glory. But before that happens, we're as blind as bats to the radical damage we are inflicting on ourselves and others. Paul reminded us that "the god of this world has blinded the minds of the unbelievers, to keep them from seeing the light of the gospel of the glory of Christ, who is the image of God" (2 Corinthians 4:4).

The gospel makes us privy to the pure, ever-brightening, all-glorious revelation that came with the death of Christ Jesus. It was this act of willing bloodshed that removed our shame and replaced it with a hope that is ongoing and ever growing, like the beam of light from an oncoming train from miles away that becomes brighter and more illuminating as it inches closer and closer. What's interesting is that the light itself technically never changes size. The wattage assigned to it is a fixed thing. The effect that the light has on us is due to its proximity. The nearer, the brighter.

I THINK NOT HAVING
A GIMMICK IS YOUR GIMMICK

AUTHENTICITY AND
INSTITUTIONALIZED HURT

Ted Kluck

My wife works in an office. It is, by and large, a great office filled with great people who are, for the most part, kind and gracious and affirming. Since she works in an office, she occasionally has meetings where they show TED Talks, which is a phenomenon that has totally escaped me being that I am (a) self-employed and (b) not on social media. Sometimes she comes home and shows me the talks if they're in any way thought provoking. TED Talks are sort of like the secular version of the evangelical conference circuit—they're slickly packaged and meant to elicit a certain reaction.

Today's talk was by a very polished former academic named Brené Brown who had that "I just crawled out of the hole of academia and peer-reviewed journals and am totally lapping up the real attention I'm getting from real people in a real audience" look about her. She was a really good speaker and storyteller. Her thesis was that quote/unquote "vulnerability" is kind of the key to everything if we define everything as love, joy, creativity, and feeling "worthy." She didn't really define vulnerability, which, in my opinion, would have been the more important thing to define. Her point, though, was that people who feel "worthy" (i.e., valued; i.e., creative; i.e., successful) are always vulnerable people, not in the sense of small-child-walking-alone-in-the-dark vulnerability, but rather being-honest-with-you-in-a-conversation vulnerability.

Caveat: For Christians, vulnerability has a completely different set of definitions and activities that go along with it, such as repentance, trusting in a God we can't see, surrendering to that God, and then being accountable to others. These are the things that, for us, comprise vulnerability. But that wasn't what she was talking about at all.

What was weird about the TED Talk context for a speech about vulnerability is that at the very moment that vulnerability becomes a tactic or a technique or a sales tool, by definition (mine or hers) it ceases to be actual vulnerability and probably toes the very fine line of manipulation. Basically what I'm saying is that if I am aware that I'm being vulnerable in order to get you to open up or like me or feel comfortable with me or buy my book or give me a five-star review or love my talk, then I am probably, on some level, screwing with you. Even if I'm not entirely aware that I'm doing it. This is the total-depravity part of the equation, which is, by the way, the part of Calvinism that makes the most sense to me. This is why I need Christ.

My wife and I value authenticity. We are often prideful about this in the sense that we're often impressed by our own cleverness in terms of how we assess people and situations with the kind of honesty and candor that counteracts an evangelical subculture that can seem treacly and fake. This is, of course, a nice way of saying that sometimes we can be obnoxious and inappropriate in the process of being authentic (and even more obnoxious about deciding who else is authentic).

But it does beg the question: In a life that is filled with so many occasions where I just have to put a smile on my face and power through the awkward family get-together or the endless staff meeting, how much of a right do I have to my own "authenticity"?

Authentic is a buzzword in evangelicalism right now (and by that I mean for the last decade), but if I'm really being "authentic" I probably say no to the people who invite themselves over to my place semi-awkwardly but who I'm too polite to turn away. Or if I say yes out of obligation, I spend the balance of the evening reading in my room. Being "authentic" means that I do actually spend the entirety of the boring staff meeting shopping for vintage football jerseys on eBay (full disclosure: I've done this).

So where does "authentic" stop and "rude" start? It's hard to say. Life brings with it many occasions in which the honorable thing to do is to honor the other people in the room (and, to a larger degree, in our lives). And we do this by not reading a book or shopping online when listening to them is less interesting. We do this by paying attention to their needs and truly trying to love them in a Christlike way. This is what we're trying to teach our kids and what we're striving to do ourselves. But is that inauthentic at some level? And, as a Christian, if like Paul I am truly ready to be "poured out" in my service to others, can I even stake a claim to my own flawed, selfish sense of authenticity?

///

One of our favorite '90s movies is Cameron Crowe's paean to Seattle, *Singles*. In the film there's this character named Steve Dunne, portrayed masterfully by Campbell Scott. Steve Dunne is sort of the college-educated "everyman." Khakis and golf shirt. Engineer. Seattle SuperSonics fan. So he goes up to this girl in a club* (Kyra Sedgwick) and says something to the effect of, "Most guys have a pickup line and most guys have a gimmick, but I've decided to just be myself." To which

---

* By the way, Alice in Chains, one of my favorite Seattle bands of all time, is playing awesomely in the background of this scene. Gosh, I miss the '90s.

Sedgwick replies, "I think not having a gimmick is your gimmick."

Authenticity-related issues are on full display tonight as we've gathered to hear a worship-guy-turned-CCM*-recording-artist-of-note play a gig at a Christian college "welcome back faculty" event. The guy is, in keeping with hipster expectations of the day, bald with a huge bushy beard and thick black-framed glasses. This is the hipster equivalent of a uniform. Everybody has this, and everybody now looks exactly the same because when half your face is obscured by a beard it kind of looks like everybody else's half-obscured face.

Anyway.

The context is a little strange because it isn't an event that people have paid actual money for, so when we finish eating and the guy comes onstage, it's unclear as to what is expected of us as an audience. Polite clapping? Participation? Standing up? Can we go home now because the meal is over? It's really confusing.

Also confusing is the particular brand of contrived authenticity happening on stage. It's the thing where the guy's shtick is so tight that every comment made that is meant to make him look real and authentic is rendered a little less real and authentic by the fact that he probably made the same comment at his

---

* Contemporary Christian Music

previous twenty-three tour stops. It's clear that the guy is really good at being onstage, but it's almost like he's *too* good onstage. He's gotten so good at looking unguarded that he has almost become the definition of guardedness. The result is a really good-looking guy who is really good at playing guitar and with whom the audience makes very little actual connection. It's a fascinating dynamic.

I think it's the reason why truly great performers—guys like Andy Kaufman and Iggy Pop—changed their approach the very *moment* they got comfortable with their previous approach. At whatever point the jokes or songs feel canned and are used to manipulate an audience, it's time for new material. When Jim Carrey, as a standup, grew tired of doing the impressions that his audiences had grown to love, he once did a bit where he played a cockroach trying to avoid a vacuum cleaner and just sort of crawled around onstage for fifteen minutes. Weirdly, I respect this.

There's a fine line between honesty and shtick. And it's the reason why people who play music for a living should probably stick to just playing music in these contexts. But it's clear, with this guy, that the banter is sort of part of the deal. He makes the obligatory comment about his super-hot wife and how he really "scored" when she married him, which is meant to elicit in the audience a sense of, "Aww, what a great guy." Ditto for the video clips of his kids that come on the overhead monitors. Call me a curmudgeon but I think there's almost nothing cheaper than using your toddlers to elicit an "Aww, isn't he a great dad!" from the audience. (Note: I've done this a few times and have always felt like a dirtbag for it.) What's weird is that I'm not that old but I can point to numerous examples of other pastors/speakers/performers doing the *exact* same thing to their audiences. What they're doing is contriving authenticity and using it as a lever.

Granted, maybe the majority of the audience doesn't notice or doesn't care. But I always notice when this is being done to me in a Christian context, and it almost always makes me angry.

Part of the nature of life in the twenty-first century is that we now *expect* a sense of intimacy with our performers that was previously nonexistent. The fact that I can go home from the awkward worship gig/concert and follow this guy on Twitter and "friend" him on Facebook makes me feel as though I have some kind of relationship with him that is, in reality, just a convenient way for him to let me know when he has a new product for me to buy. In reality we are no closer friends than strangers passing on a sidewalk. I am no one to him in the same way that most of my readers are no one to me.

I think this contrived intimacy in the name of "platform building" is one of the most dangerous dynamics on the current evangelical horizon.

///

My friend, whom I'm meeting at a local coffee shop, is at first glance "admissions brochure kid" for the Christian college he used to attend and at which I used to teach. He is tall, blond, and impeccably dressed. We're meeting for coffee because we're friends now, which is one of the added benefits to teaching in a university setting. The students with whom you make meaningful connections often become friends for life.

"When I think back on school," he says, "I usually feel like I screwed the whole thing up." This is, of course, shocking to me because at a distance it looked as if he was owning the small Grand Rapids campus in a way that other students only wished they could. We talk for a minute about the ways in which one could quantifiably "screw up" that kind of scenario—apostasy, huge moral failure of one kind or another, or massively squandering your parents' money by quitting before you get your degree.

"You didn't do any of those things," I explain. "From where I sit, I think it was a massive success."

"But the thing is," he says, "when he [the university president] gets up for the first chapel of the year and says that this will be the best four years of your life and you will make lifelong friends, I feel like I'm screwing it up because that isn't necessarily true for me. He says that every day you can either survive or thrive. I spent a lot of days just surviving."

"He's a fund-raiser," I explain, "in the way that all university presidents are fund-raisers. It's his job to say things like that, but in doing so he doesn't realize that he's adding a tremendous weight of pressure to a thing (moving away from home, starting college, embarking on a career) that's already loaded with all kinds of anxiety and pressure and nervousness." The survive-or-thrive thing is, in a sense, fortune-cookie wisdom. It's a nice thought. It makes sense, I guess, as a thing to say to a roomful of potentially lazy college students. But still, there are a lot of biblical examples of people just surviving for a season, sometimes long seasons.

We ponder, for a moment, how a Christian college could actually recruit students and market itself if the leaders didn't make these sorts of utopian promises, if they basically said, "We're going to teach good classes and give you a nice place to live but without the added pressure of feeling like you need to lock down a best friend, a spouse, and the memories of a lifetime here."

What's interesting is that his older brother was even more of an Admissions Brochure Superstar than he was (outgoing, fashionable, and so on), and he felt many of the same things in terms of emptiness and anxiety. It was incredibly helpful for me, even in my late thirties, to hear that life wasn't one big continuous (but always appropriate) party for the BMOC (Big Man on Campus) of a Christian college. So if it's difficult for everybody (at some level), why are we selling the dream that it won't be?

And while a Christian college isn't the same as church, it is filled with future church members and church leaders who are having Utopia drilled into their heads from the day of the first chapel to the day they graduate. Christian colleges, as well as modern churches, seem to be in the business of creating new Jerusalems (slick, successful, impressive, and full of amenities). But the Bible reminds us that the good things, the godly things of this world, usually come out of the Nazareths (under-resourced, under-impressive, under-the-radar). "God always works through the men or the boys nobody wanted, through the women or girls nobody wanted," Timothy Keller wrote in *Encounters with Jesus.* "Never the one from Jerusalem, as it were, always the one from Nazareth."[13]

Christian colleges and modern churches are in the Jerusalem business. I visited one West Michigan Christian college recently that boasted a climbing wall, an Olympic-quality natatorium with a luxury box for recruiting, and the crown jewel of the athletic department—a five-thousand-seat arena that puts most of the arenas in the Mid-American Conference and the Big Ten to shame. All those things are nice, and I enjoyed them while I was on campus speaking at a conference. And to some degree the school is just catering to a clientele (progeny of moneyed West Michiganders) who have come to expect such swankiness. But I couldn't shake the feeling that what I was seeing was both (a) ridiculous and (b) bound to set students up for a postcollegiate feeling of disappointment and failure when they discover that, frankly, most of life just isn't that nice. It also sort of glosses over what should be central to the Christian college (or church) experience: the gospel. And understanding the gospel is impossible without a fundamental understanding of our own sinfulness.

"Sin is looking to something else, besides God, for your salvation," wrote Keller. He added later, "We must understand that we are stained, that we have guilt and shame, and we need to be purified—not conned into believing it doesn't exist."[14] So perhaps, as institutions, we lull people into a false sense of security. We give them four years (or, in the case of a church, a lifetime) of entertainment, swank amenities, and empty promises all while, as J. C. Ryle chillingly wrote, "they trifle their souls into hell."[15]

Now, to be fair, starting each year with a chapel reminding us that we are all sinners whose hearts are sick and whose motives are untrustworthy isn't exactly going to get parents excited and encourage donors to open their checkbooks. I get that.

But institutionally we are setting people up for failure, hurt, and despair if we don't give them the meat and marrow of the gospel.

Having found the job market tougher than he expected, my friend is living back at home and is seeing a counselor. I tell him I admire him for facing it head-on and battling it when, at some level, constant motion and activity could have, in this case, actually been the easier road.

"By the time you get to your late thirties, you know how many people are going to remember that you were unemployed for two months after college?" I ask.

My friend has nothing.

"Zero," I explain. "It feels like a big deal now because everybody is posting their first pictures of their offices and their suits on Twitter."

"I look at my friends' social media feeds and it's basically a highlight reel for their lives," he says. "Again, I feel like I'm screwing something up." And again, I remind him that if he is loving God with all his heart and loving his neighbor, then he is not screwing up. And that constant activity (and then the curating of said activity online) is often a hedge against dealing with the emptiness and joylessness that is actually there. There's always another overseas trip that can be booked or another party to be documented. We've made it very easy for people to never deal with their issues by making it very easy for them to be perpetually busy.

The question then becomes, how do we deal with these institution-related hurts in a godly way? Harboring bitterness toward a Christian college that, if anything, just has an unreasonable culture and/or marketing problem isn't the answer.

Perhaps the answer lies in rethinking our expectations. What if instead of promising students (and check-writing parents) the most amazing four years of their lives, we acknowledged that the four years they're about to experience will probably be filled with ups and downs and hurts because the people with whom they'll be sharing dorm rooms, eating meals, and playing guitar shirtless under a tree (there is *always* that guy at a Christian college) are all sinners.

What if we urged students to be part of a community that, instead of promoting perfection, urged them to seek and grant forgiveness on a regular basis? To be the kind of campus that says, "I'm genuinely sorry" and "I forgive you"?

8

THE OIL AND DEW
OF UNITY

Ronnie Martin

Unity Matters to God

I'll never forget the illustration a pastor used years ago to describe what happens when two people in a marriage relationship decide to separate. He said it's like gluing two pieces of college-ruled paper together, letting them dry, and then trying to pull them apart. It doesn't take a wild imagination to envision the absurdity of even attempting such an arduous task. The only thing you could possibly end up with between bouts of maniacal frustration would be bits of paper with frayed edges stuck together, lying in torn fragments all over the floor. The pastor's intent behind this illustration was to provide a vivid example of the effect that divorce inflicts on two people when they've chosen to "separate" what "God has joined together."

Even though the heartrending havoc of divorce isn't the

topic of this book, the severing of relationships and the dissolution of friendships can have an effect that in some respects feels akin to the emotional wreckage of a marital breakdown. God hates divorce because it's a spiritual union that forms a mirror image of Christ's unique and sacrificial love for the church.

> And he is before all things, and in him all things hold
> together. And he is the head of the body, the church.
> He is the beginning, the firstborn from the dead, that
> in everything he might be preeminent. For in him all
> the fullness of God was pleased to dwell, and through
> him to reconcile to himself all things, whether on earth
> or in heaven, making peace by the blood of his cross.
> (Colossians 1:17–20)

Paul was describing the interconnectedness that exists between Christ, the Father, creation, the cross, and the church. He is before all things, all things hold together in Him, all the fullness of God dwells within Him, and all things are reconciled through Him. That's a lot of "things." The church is in a sense glued together with Christ to the point that when God sees us, He sees the glory of His Son's righteousness and He's well pleased to accept us and adopt us as sons and heirs. But it doesn't stop there. Our joining together is supposed to be working in tandem with the rest of Christ's body so that the church continues to grow strong in God's love: "We are to grow up in every way into him who is the head, into Christ, from whom the whole body, joined and held together by every joint with which it is equipped, when each part is working properly, makes the body grow so that it builds itself up in love" (Ephesians 4:15–16).

We've probably all experienced what it's like to drive a car when it needs new brake pads. That horrible squealing you hear every time you apply pressure to the brake pedal is the metal-on-metal relationship between your pads and rotors because your brake pads have eroded down to almost nothing. I know, you've been putting off bringing your car to the mechanic for weeks hoping it will magically repair itself, but this is not how your sad, poor, neglected auto is meant to run. No matter what kind of car you drive, it won't operate at peak performance if something like the brakes aren't working properly. In the same way, unity is the part of the engine that keeps the body of Christ running at peak performance. So without question, unity matters.

It matters to God because His Son died to unite a people that had been at fatal odds with Him. It's part and parcel of His divine blueprint. From animals and people to families and nations, God is the original architect behind our understanding of community, brotherhood, kinship, fellowship, and friendship. God Himself is the first person of an eternal community of three persons called the Trinity that represents His communal mind-set and intention for mankind. Togetherness is a God-ordained idea that existed in eternity before creation was spoken into being.

God wants us to be attached people, with our attachment to Christ being our first and primary communal bond. In John 15:5, Jesus described our union with Him by saying, "I am the vine; you are the branches. Whoever abides in me and I in him, he it is that bears much fruit, for apart from me you can do nothing." Jesus not only said that the amount of Godlike character produced in our lives is directly related to abiding with Him, but He also reminded us that we are powerless to produce anything unless we are connected to Him at the root. Our union with Christ is how we are justified, sanctified, and eventually will be glorified. The reason all men and women need this unification with Christ is because of the vast chasm of separation that was introduced by Adam in the garden.

Like a lot of people these days, my wife and I made the switch from using a cable TV service to streaming our shows through a device called a Roku. It doesn't feel any different from normal TV watching except it's dependent on the strength of our Wi-Fi connection. Usually everything works shipshape. We click the show or movie we want, wait two or three seconds for it to load up, and we're well on our way to wasting half the night. But occasionally, with no warning whatsoever, we'll be in the middle of our program and the screen will arbitrarily return to the loading screen. After we give each other a look of shocked, entitled outrage at the injustice of our life, we realize we're suffering from an interruption in our Wi-Fi.

Disunity between believers is like a brief interruption. I say "brief" because if it happens between two people Christ has saved, then it won't be something that lasts forever, even if it extends through the entirety of this life. But what is the catalyst for our disunity? When you look at the way some of your own relationships have suffered through moments of breakage and fracturing, what are some of the causes you can pinpoint? Does a lack of repentance over your pride, selfishness, anger, impatience, unforgiveness, gossip, and bitterness ring some bells?

The problem with the sins I just listed is how acceptable and easily justifiable they've become within the landscape of evangelical churches that have been vastly influenced and infected by relativistic, postmodern ways of thinking. In his book *Respectable Sins,* Jerry Bridges wrote, "Sin is a spiritual and moral malignancy. Left unchecked, it can spread throughout our entire inner being and contaminate every area of our lives. Even worse, it often will 'metastasize' from us into the lives of other believers around us."[16]

This metastasizing effect Bridges was talking about is what causes our relationships in the church to crack and split and become like fragmented pieces of shattered glass. Glass is not meant to be broken in a million pieces all over the floor. It's meant to be formed into the shape of something that's useful for the function for which it was intended. Christ is preparing us to function as a radiant bride who is joyfully waiting in anticipation to be unified to her risen and resplendent groom. Unity should be our heart because it's God's heart.

We also strive for unity because it gives testimony of Christ to the world.

UNITY FOR THE SAKE OF CHRIST

There was a small row of houses not far from me that were recently bulldozed over to make way for a shiny new drug and convenience store. At the risk of sounding like some hardened advocate for gentrification, these houses were old, dilapidated, slightly haunted-looking abodes that had become an unsightly presence along one of the main roads in the town. Years of neglect had left trails of white paint peeling off the once-beautiful wood sidings that were now splitting down the center and hanging off the exposed framing. Every part of the houses seemed pulled apart and disconnected from other parts. If you stood back far enough and viewed them from a distance, the houses appeared cute, quaint, and very much "together," but if you moved closer, the horrified look on your face would have revealed your opinion that they should be condemned.

I use this analogy to give a simple illustration of how sin

dismantles and disfigures the face of our relationships. Sin comes from a neglect in all of us to keep God's laws by obeying the lawgiver perfectly and without fail. Failure to keep God's law is what grounds us in worldliness and judgment against our brothers and sisters. When we sin against others, we are acting as their judge. We are saying, "I'm the one who deserves to punish you, treat you unfairly, enact vindication against you, and condemn you." Hurting someone in the church is a denial of the One we go to church to worship, who is "Lord both of the dead and of the living" (Romans 14:9).

James, the brother of Jesus, warned against worldly sin when he said, "There is only one lawgiver and judge, he who is able to save and to destroy. But who are you to judge your neighbor?" (James 4:12).

Failing to obey the lawgiver creates a separation between God and man that leads to condemnation. And yet, on the cross, Jesus healed that separation, removed the condemnation, laid a new foundation, and started construction on a new house called the church that He continues to slowly and steadily build into an indestructible fortress that hell has no power to destroy. It's a structure that displays the handiwork of Christ and His ability to make old things new and tie together what has been torn apart. Everyone Christ detaches from the tree of death that Adam ate from is now a new branch connected to a new tree with Jesus as its vine. At one point we were all disconnected from Christ and companions with death, but at the cross that association was severed and we are now reconnected by a new union with Christ.

This togetherness, this unity of heart, soul, and mind with Christ and among followers of Christ is not really presented as an option. Jesus never said, "Hey, guys, why can't we all just get along because I hate it when we all fight?" Instead, He did the only thing nobody was able to do to restore unity. He lived a perfect life in this world to defeat the disunity of death that awaited mankind in the next world.

The death and resurrection of Jesus is like a candle being lit in the darkest corner of the darkest cave in the lowest point of the earth, where everything this solitary beam of light touches will be unable to hide, unable to remain blind, and unable to be unaffected any longer.

All around us are dark, painful portraits of glaring disunity. The past two years will likely be remembered as a hallmark in church history, as the reemergence of unsettled racial tension, the eye-opening atrocities of abortion, and the radical redefinitions of marriage have created new lanes for the church to sort through and learn to travel down. Although it's not my intention to delve into the controversies each of these issues brings about, it's not difficult to see the level of embarrassing disunity and ugliness that has risen to the surface of the American church every time we're confronted with how to respond to them. The question that needs to be asked is, "Who do you follow?" If it's Jesus, then we follow Him down a road paved with mercy, grace, love, humility, and self-sacrifice. These are the kinds of godly fruits that characterize Christ's beautiful and blood-bought unity. Of course, unity is not all inclusive, but it does include being intentional about pleasing God over man by loving what God loves and hating what God hates. So why should we strive for unity? Because unity says something about Jesus, whom God sent to fill in the crevices of division that had been created by our sin.

As truly saved, sanctified, and adopted "church people," we've been unified with Jesus. That means we share a particular connectedness with everyone else who has been unified with Him. So what does unity mean for those embroiled in personally hurtful examples of disunity? Of all the subjects the apostle Paul could have addressed as he began to pen his rather long letter to the church in Corinth, the first one he brought up was, you guessed it, division in the church.

AGREE TO AGREE

You don't have to read too far into Paul's letter to the Corinthian church to see that churches have not come too far in terms of spiritual maturity. Paul opened his letter by acknowledging that this was a legitimate church "because of the grace of God that

was given you in Christ Jesus, that in every way you were en-
riched in him in all speech and all knowledge—even as the
testimony about Christ was confirmed among you—so that
you are not lacking in any gift, as you wait for the revealing of
our Lord Jesus Christ, who will sustain you to the end, guiltless
in the day of our Lord Jesus Christ" (1 Corinthians 1:4–8).

This was a church that had met Jesus, knew Jesus, gave
testimony of Him, was being sanctified in Him, and had not
been shortchanged or had any spiritual need withheld that
would keep them from growing and thriving in Christ until He
returned. Paul went on to affirm the legitimacy of their calling
when he said, "God is faithful, by whom you were called into
the fellowship of his Son, Jesus Christ our Lord" (verse 9).

In some ways the Corinthian church was similar to our
modern-day megachurch multiplexes. The details are obviously
different, but the foundations are the same. Today we have un-
questionably great facilities that resemble something between a
concert venue, basketball arena, and fun zone trampoline park.
We have pastoral staffs that work around the clock to provide
personal and passionate preaching, daring and dynamic worship, and youth programs that rival the Video Music Awards on
MTV every September. Everything seems to run as faultless
and fluid as the clock on the big screen that counts down to the
start of the first service every Sunday morning.

All sarcasm aside (and nothing against larger churches,

they're simply a fun, easy target), the Corinthian church probably appeared solid from a multitude of perspectives. The nuts and bolts seemed secure and screwed in properly. But that wasn't the case at all.

Paul didn't waste a minute getting right to the heart of the matter: "I appeal to you, brothers, by the name of our Lord Jesus Christ, that all of you agree, and that there be no divisions among you, but that you be united in the same mind and the same judgment" (1:10).

Let's not miss how Paul started his appeal: "by the name of our Lord Jesus Christ." Notice what he didn't say. There was no appeal made for them to come together in the name of friendship, theology, or their combined love for the NFL draft and fantasy football leagues. His appeal was "by the name of our Lord Jesus Christ." The question Paul was asking in his appeal was, "Who is Lord over your life?" Who is Lord over the deep confines of your mind? Who is Lord over the sensitive fragility of your heart? If Jesus is Lord, then your actions will be bright, glittering, blinding reflections of Him.

Without Christ as the center of our lives and the object of our motivations, there are innumerable things for us to be divided over, to fight about, and to be perpetually swimming in a pool of discontentment over. This is what happened to the Corinthians. Divisions had started to surface, and instead of calling on the name of the One responsible for bridging the ultimate gap between God and man, they let their opinions and ambitions spiral into states of silliness and separation.

What Paul was driving at here is that the motivation for their unity with one another had to be the unity they had in Christ as the Lord over their lives, master over their hearts, and captain over their souls. The name of Jesus reminds us that our selfish desires have been claimed and redeemed by the act of a selfless Savior. It's unity with one another within the greater union of Christ that doesn't allow us the option of angrily splintering over insubstantial differences or shallow disagreements.

TOGETHER FOREVER

One of the results of our petty fighting and small-minded arguments is that it often leads to physical separation. Unresolved differences among church members can lead to awkward avoidances on Sundays at best and abrupt exits from the church body at worst.

But there's a subtle irony at play here when we consider what it is we're saying as we cave in to irreconcilable differences. The church is a forever institution. Everybody who transfers from the kingdom of the world into the kingdom of heaven becomes part of an eternal community of saved sinners. Paul said, "To us who are being saved it is the power of God" (1 Corinthians 1:18).

It was Christ's singular act of divine power that allowed for the possibility of eternal rescue. Being saved is not simply a momentary action where God removes us from the flames so that He can turn them to low and then place us back in them. After all, God didn't reduce the flames of hell for us; He rescued us from them! Can you imagine diving into a pool to save a family member who is drowning and then, right after performing mouth-to-mouth, kicking him back in the water?

Everyone has different stories of rescue, but in a sense they're all the same story. Some were saved from drug abuse, alcohol addiction, slavery to porn, first-degree murder, or adulterous affairs, while others were saved from anger, pride, gossip, and selfishness. All those sins are equally damning and in need of gospel reconciliation between God and man, which means all rescued repenters are heading toward a shared future. Whatever has been severed here will be joined together in heaven. Whatever is broken here will be repaired in eternity. Shouldn't our lives be an early rehearsal for the never-ending drama that will be heaven? Or should we simply throw up our hands and resolve that on this side of heaven, differences will be exaggerated, fractures will occur, and disunity among the brethren will be a woeful inevitability? Shouldn't our future destination play a role in our current situation, or are we condemned to allow the past to be our victor? For once, can't we just agree to agree?

THE BEAUTY OF UNITY

Unity is like a settled fluidness. It's like a body of water that moves but remains resolutely in its location. Or like snow-capped mountains planted like pillars in the far-off but visible landscape. There's an immovability, a constancy, a kind of motionless joy where every time we set our sights on these impenetrable shapes we know they'll continue to inhabit the fullness they embody.

There's an almost artistic beauty and creative wonder when God plants an eagerness to "maintain the unity of the Spirit in the bond of peace" in the hearts of His children (Ephesians 4:3). There's a portrait of heaven, painted in the breathing, walking, eating, living, and being of souls who physically embody the very attributes of God. Paul went on to say, "There is one body and one Spirit—just as you were called to the one hope that belongs to your call—one Lord, one faith, one baptism, one God and Father of all, who is over all and through all and in all (verses 4–6).

Do you see the gloriousness of unity? Like billows of clouds in the ripeness of autumn, falling effortlessly into one another to form fathomless shapes of heart-stopping splendor. God designed community to be diversely unified as the church evolves under the banner of a singularly blessed hope! Like a family during the holidays under one roof, with one fire in the hearth to warm them all, one table to share the bounty among all, and one love between father, mother, and siblings to serve all. How can we not be eager to "maintain the unity of the Spirit in the bond of peace"?

We've taken a fully illustrated, full-color, beautifully bound chronicle of Christ's church and replaced it with a thin, grainy, black-and-white newspaper edition that leaves a residue of black dye on our hands because the hope of our call has been subdued by the hindrances of our fall. It's not that we've lost our desire to be unified; it's that we've lost the greater desire for God.

Whenever we let our minds gravitate to the hurt that's been leveled at us, we are simultaneously forgetting the hope that Christ extended to us on the cross. Christ is saying, "Look at how much I've forgiven for you to be hidden under the universe-sized umbrella of my righteousness!" And yet, with smallness of mind, we hide under a child-sized umbrella, complaining about the occasional drops of rain that touch our skin and soak through our clothing.

Unity happens when repentance is pursued regardless of the outcome of the relational detachment we've experienced. God is first and foremost concerned with our unity to Him. Sins such as pride and bitterness keep us separated from God before they separate us from another church member.

There's a beauty to us striving to be unified. The psalmist described it as good and pleasant!

Behold, how good and pleasant it is
   when brothers dwell in unity!
It is like the precious oil on the head,
   running down on the beard,
on the beard of Aaron,
   running down on the collar of his robes!
It is like the dew of Hermon,
   which falls on the mountains of Zion!
For there the LORD has commanded the blessing,
   life forevermore. (Psalm 133)

Brothers and sisters, should we give the devil due opportunity to drag us back into our former depravity of disunity that Christ came to deliver us from? Would we ignore the mission of Christ Himself, which the apostle John clearly informed us of when he said, "The reason the Son of God appeared was to destroy the works of the devil" (1 John 3:8)? Have we not been united in holiness under the saving and sanctifying blood work of Jesus? Are we not equally dependent on the same God for the same measure of mercy, grace, and forgiveness that He gives to all who repent of their disunity with Him? The pain we experience over disunity in the church will never be as great as the pain Christ experienced and endured to build His unified church.

We would do better to obey the words of Paul, who instructed the church of Ephesus to "speak the truth with his neighbor" (Ephesians 4:25), "be angry and do not sin" (verse 26), "let the thief no longer steal" (verse 28), "let no corrupting talk come out of your mouths" (verse 29), "do not grieve the Holy Spirit of God" (verse 30), and "let all bitterness and wrath and anger and clamor and slander be put away from you" (verse 31). Why? Because "we are members one of another" (verse 25), and we should "give no opportunity to the devil" (verse 27) but "labor, doing honest work with [our] own hands, so that [we] may have something to share with anyone in need" (verse 28). We should "give grace" (verse 29) and "be kind to one another, tenderhearted, forgiving one another, as God in Christ forgave [us]" (verse 32).

When we sacrifice for the sake of unity, we are known by the world as people who are known by God: "By this all people will know that you are my disciples, if you have love for one another" (John 13:35).

CLOSING ADDRESS

Is there ever a precedent for any form of disunity? Do personalities play a part in the complexities that cause people to come apart at the seams? We are not called to have the same intimacy or relationship with everyone we come into contact with in our local church, are we? Isn't it possible that hurtful things happen because sometimes people are just not compatible? Certainly! When you get to the end of many of the apostle Paul's letters, you hear him mention and show gratitude for many of his closest friends who supported, encouraged, loved, and cared for him. Is it possible that there was ever any conflict between them, that hurtful things were said, and that they experienced moments of repentance and forgiveness? We're given insight into one particular moment, a near legendary breakup scene in Acts 15 when Barnabas and Paul had to part ways due to a disagreement they had over a young apprentice by the name of John Mark.

Barnabas wanted to take John Mark with them on their journey. Paul was against it because at some point on an earlier excursion, John Mark had bailed on them and they had to continue the tour without him. The text says,

> And there arose a sharp disagreement, so that they
> separated from each other. Barnabas took Mark with
> him and sailed away to Cyprus, but Paul chose Silas and
> departed, having been commended by the brothers to
> the grace of the Lord. And he went through Syria and
> Cilicia, strengthening the churches. (Acts 15:39–41)

Now there's some evidence in the book of 2 Timothy that Paul and John Mark later reconciled. Paul said, "Get Mark and bring him with you, for he is very useful to me for ministry" (4:11). How about Barnabas? We're never really told. The reality is that there are some people in the church we're never going to get along great with or become close friends with, and we'll probably continue to struggle with them as long as we're around them. It's important for us to remember that God has sovereignly placed people in our lives, and us in theirs, to do a sanctifying work in us that will produce a greater fruit and a more abiding joy. What we never heard from Paul was any gossip, slander, or complaining against Barnabas because they happened to disagree and parted ways. God used their disagreement to spread them out and reach more people than they could have had they stayed together.

What we do know is that Paul preached a theology of unity very strongly and specifically to the church, and he wrote some very insightful and motivating words about it to churches. Here's how Paul began his thoughts on unity with the Ephesians:

> I therefore, a prisoner for the Lord, urge you to walk in
> a manner worthy of the calling to which you have been
> called, with all humility and gentleness, with patience,
> bearing with one another in love, eager to maintain the
> unity of the Spirit in the bond of peace. (4:1–3)

RESTORATION

Ted Kluck

My new office building looks like Rhett Butler's mansion, as do all buildings in the South that take themselves seriously. I've taken a new job teaching at a Christian university and am moving into my new office and trying to adjust to the heat, which feels like it's about 150 degrees with 100 percent humidity. Living here is like always running a low-grade fever. On my way out of the office with a few empty book boxes, I run into the new dean of religion, a guy just a few years older than me. He has a pickup truck filled completely with boxes of books and yet another pull-behind trailer, also filled to the brim with meticulously labeled book boxes. In an academic, book-measuring contest, I would lose miserably.

"Ted Kluck. You're not emergent, but you love the church," he says, cleverly. It is, of course, exactly the right thing to say at the right time because it acknowledges some accomplishments of mine while also acknowledging (without saying it) the fact that those accomplishments took place awhile ago and are rendered somehow less impressive by the passage of time. I have a new appreciation for how child stars must feel after they grow up. It's also the perfect thing to say because there is no comfortable comeback for me. There is no equally clever thing to say in return. I just chuckle uncomfortably and say, "Yeah," while extending a hand.

This guy is part of a somewhat new breed of semihipster intellectuals in that while he has the doctorate and several thousand books, he also wears the requisite bushy beard, comic-book shirt, and thick-framed glasses. He's the guy a lot of Christian guys on Twitter wish they were. And now he has a sweet job.

After meeting the dean it occurred to me that I wished he were my friend Cory Hartman.* We've been friends since undergrad at Taylor University, and I wrote about him at the end of one of the church books with Kevin DeYoung, when he was pastoring a small church filled with older folks in Passaic, New Jersey. He's now pastoring a church filled with mostly older folks in Hollidaysburg, Pennsylvania, and also has a doctorate. Cory is one of the smartest people I know and also one of the

---

* I've since hung out with the new dean some more and discovered that he is a truly awesome guy and a great addition to our campus. And while I love my friend Cory, I'm still glad this guy is here.

most unique in that while he fully embraces the tenets of Calvinism (for example, God's sovereignty in all things) he also has an equally robust affection for and attentiveness to the mysterious workings of the Holy Spirit. Within traditional neo-Calvinism (heh, contradictory?) these two categories are almost always mutually exclusive, and in fact a lot of new Calvinist types look askance at people who are too into the Holy Spirit.

So I had been planning to e-mail or text that little anecdote to Cory as a means of providing encouragement, given that my friend wants to, at some point, make the move to academia. But before I could do so, he called me with a chilling story that fills me with all the hope in the world that local church ministry and membership is worth fighting for.

On a recent morning Cory preached a sermon to his small congregation in his small church. The building looks Colonially fussy in the same way that my office building looks Rhett-Butler-Southern fussy. After the sermon, a woman in her midfifties approached him and wanted to talk. She was blue collar, had never had a salaried job, and had a variety of physical concerns. Her upbringing was nightmarish and was the sort of upbringing that makes suburbanite, upscale, Christian college–educated people like us feel soft and guilty. "If somebody made a movie of her life, you and I wouldn't watch it because it would be too depressing," Cory explained.

She had just received financial assistance from the church

and had promised to show up on Sunday. And then she actually did.

"That never happens," said Cory.

She then proceeded to tell Cory about her life and her struggles, after which my friend suggested that what she needed was salvation—a relationship with Christ. She needed to place her hope in the God of the universe and have her sins forgiven by Christ's blood. So then she sat in his empty sanctuary and prayed to receive Christ.

"That also never happens," Cory explained. "Meaning that in all my years of ministry I've never had somebody sit in the sanctuary after I preached and receive Christ."

"I feel a lightness that I've never felt," she said afterward. "I feel hopeful and free." And in her unsophisticated yet completely genuine way, she began telling others about what she'd experienced and brought a neighbor to church with her the following week—a woman in her late-thirties who had her own horrific upbringing and deep-seated troubles, one of which was the fact that in spite of taking a litany of medications, she couldn't sleep. After the service, she, too, asked for a personal visit.

"She lives in the same apartment building as the other lady who had just become a believer, and we visited her there," Cory explained. It was there that the woman explained that she "hasn't felt like herself in years." To which Cory replied, "Have you ever felt like yourself?" She said no. They prayed, they read Scripture together, and they sang. All the while, the first woman—the new believer—kept chiming in with beautifully simple yet profoundly true statements like, "You just need to trust Jesus with your life."

"It was like early-church stuff, man," Cory explained, "going out two-by-two to cast out demons." That's where it got crazy. Cory explained that it was clear there were demonic forces at work in this woman's life—a feeling that was confirmed by her explanation of her family's long history with the occult.

As they spoke and prayed and read, the woman's hand and arm began to feel hot. Like searingly, uncomfortably hot. And then she began to hear voices in her head.

Note: This is the part where, as a mostly suburbanite Calvinist, I would have begun to feel a little bit uncomfortable, were it not for the fact that I trust Cory completely. I know the depth of his commitment to Christ because we have walked through a great many things together. I also believe him because he has been completely honest with me about his own struggles, so why would he not also be completely honest about this?

"What were the voices saying?" I asked.

"They said, 'I am Legion, for we are many,'" he replied. At this point in the conversation I got chills, and the hairs stood up on the back of my neck. I felt completely terrified yet unwaveringly safe in the arms of the living God. I also felt as though I was about to have my mind blown by the power of that God. This is not a woman who would have ever read the book of Mark or had the ability, in and of herself, to call up that particular phrase.

In Mark 5 Jesus healed a demon-possessed man:

They went across the lake to the region of the Gerasenes. When Jesus got out of the boat, a man with an impure spirit came from the tombs to meet him. This man lived in the tombs, and no one could bind him anymore, not even with a chain. For he had often been chained hand and foot, but he tore the chains apart and broke the irons on his feet. No one was strong enough to subdue him. Night and day among the tombs and in the hills he would cry out and cut himself with stones.

When he saw Jesus from a distance, he ran and fell on his knees in front of him. He shouted at the top of his voice, "What do you want with me, Jesus, Son of the Most High God? In God's name don't torture me!" For Jesus had said to him, "Come out of this man, you impure spirit!"

Then Jesus asked him, "What is your name?"

"My name is Legion," he replied, "for we are many." And he begged Jesus again and again not to send them out of the area.

A large herd of pigs was feeding on the nearby hillside. The demons begged Jesus, "Send us among the pigs; allow us to go into them." He gave them permission, and the impure spirits came out and went into the pigs. The herd, about two thousand in number, rushed down the steep bank into the lake and were drowned.

Those tending the pigs ran off and reported this in the town and countryside, and the people went out to see what had happened. (verses 1–14)

Cory explained that as they talked and prayed, the demons began to threaten him and his family, saying they would get him at his point of weakness. "Of course I'm weak," he prayed, "but I'm strong in the power of Christ. And you can do nothing to me outside what my Lord ordains." As they prayed, the voices began to subside, and the young woman's fear was replaced by a sense of calm. She, too, felt a lightness and joy that had never been there before. They sang "Amazing Grace" together and the woman saw, in her mind's eye, the points in her life when the demons had entered her. But she also felt the peace that they had departed and no longer held any power over her.

By the end of the story I was weeping. I wept at God's goodness and power and at the fact that He would use my ordinary friend and his even more ordinary new convert as the conduits for it.

After pulling myself together, I said, "Dude, that doesn't happen in academia." It doesn't. Academia is great for many reasons. It's necessary and good for people to study and conference and white-paper. But still, what Cory described doesn't happen there, and it really doesn't happen on the conference/publishing/celebrity circuit either. It happens in places where people are humbled and broken, not where people are receiving accolades and being exalted.

"It sounds to me like an example of the Lord using the weak to shame the strong," I said.

"Amen, brother."

Warrior and the Long Road of Forgiveness

I was introduced to the film *Warrior,* starring Nick Nolte and Tom Hardy, by my pastor and friend Norm Dufrin. He introduced it to me because he knows I like fighting, but also because the film is more than just a *Rocky*-style fight movie. It certainly isn't a Christian film in the conventional sense of the term. But it has manifestly Christian values and, I think, much to teach about what repentance and forgiveness and grace can look like in human terms.

In very simple terms, forgiveness is hard because we're not Christ. But forgiveness is possible because we're made in His image. Without God's common grace, there would be no forgiveness in this world, by anybody. And while *Warrior* is about mixed martial arts (MMA), it is about MMA in the same way that *Friday Night Lights* is just about football. Meaning that it's not really about MMA.

Warrior is about a broken family. They're broken because of a not-fully-disclosed lifetime of drinking and (ostensibly) abuse that Paddy Conlon (Nick Nolte's character) inflicted on his children. His children are both wrestlers that he trained, and they are both very successful at it. They both hate their father and are estranged from each other until they (spoiler alert) find themselves in the same mixed martial arts tournament.

Tommy Conlon (Hardy) is bitter and mad at his father, mad at his brother (Joel Edgerton), and mad at the world in general. He was a marine who left the service under dubious circumstances. His brother, Brendan (Edgerton), is a schoolteacher in Philly and moonlights as a low-rent MMA fighter. He's about to lose his home to foreclosure. Their father (Nolte) is a recovering alcoholic going on one thousand days of sobriety. Tommy approaches his father because his father, while bad at fathering, was very good at training him for battle.

The Importance of Hanging in There (for the Offending Party)

The Nolte character is genuinely broken and tearfully and humbly seeks the forgiveness of both his boys. They don't give it. But because he loves his boys, he takes it. He takes their passive-aggressive comments and their aggressive-aggressive comments. He risks the heartache of trying to reach out to them and being rebuffed. He quietly hangs around and hangs in. He wants to be near his boys. He is broken and sad, but he takes it.

The Importance of Realistic Expectations (for the Offending Party)

The boys' father doesn't expect to be fully reinstated as Father and Head of the Household the moment his sons walk back into his life. He doesn't expect things to go back to the way they were right away. He acknowledges, in fact, that they will probably never go back to the way they were. He maintains hope, but he's smart enough to not ask for the moon because it would be insulting and inappropriate to do so.

Sometimes when we offend and then have our brokenness/ redemption moment, we expect the whole world to get on board immediately. We want things to immediately go back to a preoffense state. But this difficult dynamic is summed up well in the film by Edgerton's character when he says, "Pop, I forgive you, but I don't trust you."

The Importance of Being Broken (for Both Parties, but Especially the Offended Party)

For each character in the film, there is no chance of extending or receiving grace until he sees the other completely broken and vulnerable. The hardened and embittered Tommy doesn't relent until he sees his father physically broken, in the grips of a relapse. Then he finally relents and holds him, caring for him. It is one of the beautiful moments in a film that is really barbaric at times. I am not an MMA fan. I don't love the chest-beating, Tapout T-shirt–style bravado of a fight game that happens, literally, inside a chain-link fence. It may be the ultimate hypocritical pot-calling-the-kettle-black scenario for me (as a football player and once-in-a-while boxer) to say that I find the sport base and barbaric. But I do. And yet the film works because of the forgiveness element.

Sometimes people who have been hurt hold on to it because it gives them leverage. They feel that withholding forgiveness and hope is the only power they have. One of the humblest and godliest things an offended person can do is acknowledge that, in Christ, there is a shred of hope. That in Christ all things can somehow be made new. This is extremely hard to do.

Tommy, himself, doesn't relent and forgive until he is physically broken in the ring by his brother. It is only in the embrace of a submission hold, with his brother saying, "I'm sorry and I love you," that Tommy finally taps out, both literally and figuratively. In that moment he gives up on being mad. He gives up on grinding the very large and in many ways legitimate ax that he has been grinding for years, vis-à-vis his father and brother and the unfairness of life. He gives up. He forgives.

And that's where the movie ends. It doesn't go into what happens tomorrow. It doesn't answer the question of "How often are we going to hang out?" or "What will it look like at Christmas?" It ends, simply, with a very important promise to forgive.

In his beautiful essay *On Forgiveness,* C. S. Lewis wrote, "We believe that God forgives us our sins; but also that He will not do so unless we forgive other people their sins against us. There is no doubt about the second part of this statement. It is in the Lord's Prayer; it was emphatically stated by our Lord. If you don't forgive you will not be forgiven."[17]

This is precisely why Christianity feels like foolishness and audacity to the world—the idea that in order to fully forgive you for the horrible thing you did to me, I have to also be fully aware of my *own* horribleness, of the deep darkness, sin history, and sin potential in my own heart. But at the same time that I am fully aware of this, I am also able to live a joyful and fun life, for I am at the same time fully aware that Christ paid the penalty for all my deep darkness, sin history, and sin potential. The result is staggering. Literally. The result is what makes men tremble at the power and goodness of the living God.

"Forgiveness," wrote Lewis, "says, Yes, you have done this thing, but I accept your apology; I will never hold it against you and everything between us two will be exactly as it was before."[18]

If you have ever been on the receiving end of forgiveness like this you have, no doubt, been staggered by it. It has probably brought you to your knees and you have been filled with joy and gratitude. I know I have. I have sat in front of people who have forgiven me in this way and wept at their goodness—a goodness enabled only by the fact that we share the love of Christ in common.

This book opened with a fairy-tale story about my friend's move from West Coast to Midwest, from rock star to pastor, and from honeymoon phase to hard reality. We're now a few years out. He has planted a church, and my reason for ever going to MWT again is gone (meaning, I've finished my degree and it's hard to find time to go there). Considering that he's a few years past the pain, I asked him to talk about the challenges and sin-related pitfalls that God revealed to him in this situation (for example, pride, anger, jealousy, resentment, hopelessness, worry, and so on).

"I think pride and anger were probably the major challenges as I navigated the hurtful waters I experienced," he wrote. "Being hurt by a church while serving on staff carries some unique weight. I had expectations for the 'way things should be' and when those expectations weren't met, the bitterness crept in. It started feeling extremely claustrophobic, like I was trapped in a very small space with no room to move and no light to see anything clearly anymore."

It is an apt description of bitterness in its ability to choke out the light. When we're in the midst of it, it feels like a home—a bad, dysfunctional home, but a home nonetheless. Not surprisingly, much of Ronnie's bitterness found its root in pride, in the sense that we expect and feel that we deserve one thing and then are shocked and angry when we get another.

"Like most crisis situations, hindsight reveals much," he continued. "Pride was undoubtedly one of the major ingredients that contributed to the spiraling process. I'd found myself in what felt like a hopeless scenario before an onslaught of undealt-with sins like anger, jealousy, resentment, and worry started consuming me. All those emotions started wreaking havoc on my heart. It was hard not to feel like a victim, even though I knew I wasn't completely innocent. I felt betrayed, even though in my heart I knew others could lay a similar claim on me. I felt like I'd been marginalized, but I knew that wasn't the intention of those who I felt were ignoring me. There was a level of neglect that caused me to become immersed in self-pity, but much of it was fueled by pride and selfish ambition, like the book of James reminds us.

"James 3:13–16 says, 'Who is wise and understanding among you? Let them show it by their good life, by deeds done in the humility that comes from wisdom. But if you harbor bitter envy and selfish ambition in your hearts, do not boast about it or deny the truth. Such "wisdom" does not come down from heaven but is earthly, unspiritual, demonic. For where you have envy and selfish ambition, there you find disorder and every evil practice.' How often are our deeds done from a place of selfish ambition and vain conceit? Of wanting to create the 'perfect' church culture in our own image?

"There was some real truth in everything I'm describing, but God puts a mirror up during these times to reveal your sin as being the same model/different version of the sin you feel hurt by," Ronnie explained. "And then He uses it to draw you to repentance, because these were things that existed long before they were exposed here."

I asked Ronnie how he finally resolved or dealt with the

issue, cognizant of the fact that resolution may be an ongoing process and that there may be multiple "right" ways to resolve this issue.

"Sadly enough, the issue went two years with absolutely no resolution," he said honestly. "I had lost all contact. I felt like God had dealt severely with me in a multitude of ways, but none of it had included any face-to-face attempts at reconciliation. Finally, after two years, God opened a door for me to approach the man I felt was responsible for my pain, and He allowed me to go to him and ask forgiveness for the anger and bitterness that I'd let settle into the recesses of my heart. It was about me living out the gospel that I preached every week. Unfortunately, it wasn't received incredibly well, but I thought I had done what Paul called us to do in Romans 12:18 when he said, 'As far as it depends on you, live at peace with everyone.'

"To the best of my ability, I repented for the things I thought I could repent for and prayed that God would give me the grace to move forward in my heart and mind, regardless of whether that repentance was ever reciprocated. By God's grace, I received an e-mail the next morning in which this man told me that the Spirit had convicted him of his sin and that he wanted to ask for my forgiveness. There was nothing left to do now but receive and rejoice! It was like in one moment everything went from darkness to light. Having said that, I don't know that resolution is still not an ongoing process. Some wounds go incredibly deep, but I'm thankful that the Spirit has begun some spiritual surgery in me."

It occurs to me that God is deeply glorified in these stories of restoration and that the restoration isn't possible without first feeling a deep and profound sense of pain and disillusionment. Not that we ever *want* the pain per se, but Ronnie's story reminds me that God is manifestly good and active in the midst of it. And that He can redeem it. He can redeem the years the locusts have eaten. I asked Ronnie how "faith working through love" looks in this situation, either for him, for others, or for both.

"It's interesting, but at some point in the middle of our pain, we have to ask whether we believe the gospel, which carries with it the solution to all pain," he said. "I believe God uses these moments in our lives to test our faith to see if we are becoming people who are learning how to respond with the love of our Savior or with the love of ourselves. Pain was one of the driving forces that led me to stop holding on to the hope of personal vindication, because it was exhausting. God hadn't taken His vengeance out on me. He'd provided Christ instead, who bore God's wrath to create peace. How could I not extend that same peace I'd been given? Was my faith that thin? How could I withhold love and forgiveness as someone who had received so much of it? In the end, it wasn't important whether I received reconciliation as much as I repented for the lack of it."

James 3:17–18 reads, "But the wisdom that comes from heaven is first of all pure; then peace-loving, considerate, submissive, full of mercy and good fruit, impartial and sincere. Peacemakers who sow in peace reap a harvest of righteousness." I have seen this in my own life, in myself, but in particular in the people who have forgiven *me* for the ways I've hurt them. This forgiveness is proof that God and the gospel are real because not only have *I* been blessed by their forgiveness, but I have also seen *them* blessed in profound ways. And I have seen God bless my friend—not necessarily monetarily or with a ten-thousand-seat church but in the sense that he has peace. And in the sense that the situation, which seemed hopeless, has borne fruit.

I asked, finally, about grace—both in the midst of the trial and also moving forward. Grace being the thing about which we're all so eloquent, but which we have such trouble actually *demonstrating.*

"I think grace is the umbrella that looms large over our hurts both before and after they're dealt with," he said. "It has to go back to what Jesus did and does for us every day, namely give us what we don't deserve, which is chiefly Himself. There has to be a fundamental acknowledgment of this grace that we pray for and strive to intentionally live out as we go through any healing process in the church. The shocking thing to come to grips with is that we're not any better than the people who have hurt us, even when that hurt has been a one-way bullet fired right into our heart. Grace accounts for that by giving us the compassion of Christ to give back to our perpetrators. There's been only one innocent person in the history of mankind, and He was shown no mercy and grace so that we could be shown an eternal supply of it."

ACKNOWLEDGMENTS

Ted Kluck

I'm thankful, most of all, for the opportunity to do creative projects with my friends, which is how I consider my coauthor Ronnie Martin and my agent Andrew Wolgemuth. We have shared life together in a way that transcends manuscript pages and deal points. It's a privilege to work with these brothers in Christ.

I'm grateful, as well, for the fine folks at WaterBrook Multnomah, including Stoddy (Andrew Stoddard) for all of the encouraging e-mails and phone calls, and John Blase for making the manuscript better and saving me from myself without making me feel like a jerk (as is, perhaps, the most important function of the book editor).

To the friends who sat for interviews: Cory Hartman, Drew Penfield, Ronnie Martin, and Sean and Christy Duffy.

To my church-related friends and mentors: Peeter Lukas, Norm and Phil Dufrin, Eric Corey, Lee Tankersley, and Cory Hartman. I thank God for all of you and your families.

Finally, since this is a book about church, I want to thank the churches that have loved me, pricked my conscience when necessary, survived my sinful nature, and cared for me as an adult. I am proud to call the pastors of these churches some of my closest friends on earth. God is truly too good to me.

Cornerstone Community Church, Jackson, TN

Covenant Life Community Church, East Lansing, MI

University Reformed Church, East Lansing, MI

First Baptist Church, Hollidaysburg, PA

Judson Memorial Baptist Church, Lansing, MI

Ronnie Martin

Thank you:

To Andrew Stoddard, John Blase, and the team at Water-Brook Multnomah for making this a joyful and collaborative process.

To Andrew Wolgemuth for wisdom, support, and guidance. Incredibly grateful for your friendship!

To the elders, deacons, community group leaders, and congregation at Substance Church. It's a gracious privilege to serve you all, the bride of Christ!

To my coauthor, collaborator, and friend, Ted Kluck. Wanna write another one?

And finally, to my wife, Melissa, and daughter, Beth. Love you forever.

NOTES

1. C. S. Lewis, *The Weight of Glory* (New York: Harper-One, 2001), 134.
2. Raymond C. Ortlund Jr., *Proverbs: Wisdom that Works* (Wheaton, IL: Crossway, 2012), 134, 131.
3. Timothy Keller, *The Prodigal God* (New York: Riverhead Books, 2008), 93–94.
4. Lewis, *The Weight of Glory*, 120.
5. Lewis, *The Weight of Glory*, 122.
6. Noah Filipiak, "Research Shows 45% of Christian Singles Feel Outcast Within the Church, 3% are LGBTQ," At a Crossroads, August 19, 2015, www.atacrossroads.net /research-shows-3-of-christian-singles-are-gay-45-feel -outcast-within-the-church/. Used with permission.
7. Walter Hooper, "Introduction," in Lewis, *The Weight of Glory*, 10.
8. Tullian Tchividjian, Facebook, www.facebook.com/Pastor Tullian.
9. Dietrich Bonhoeffer, *Life Together* (New York: Harper and Row, 1954), 11.
10. Hooper, "Introduction," in Lewis, *The Weight of Glory*, 13.

11. Lewis, *The Weight of Glory,* 36.

12. Carl R. Trueman, "Mark Driscoll's Problems, and Ours: The Crisis of Leadership in American Evangelicalism," March 14, 2014, *First Things,* www.firstthings.com/web -exclusives/2014/03/mark-driscolls-problems-and-ours.

13. Timothy Keller, *Encounters with Jesus: Unexpected Answers to Life's Biggest Questions* (New York: Riverhead Books, 2015), 8.

14. Keller, *Encounters with Jesus,* 66.

15. J. C. Ryle, "The Great Battle," www.biblebb.com/files /ryle/great_battle.htm.

16. Jerry Bridges, *Respectable Sins: Confronting the Sins We Tolerate* (Colorado Springs, CO: NavPress, 2007), 23.

17. Lewis, *The Weight of Glory,* 154.

18. Lewis, *The Weight of Glory,* 154–55.